Grieve

Stories and Poems about Grief and Loss

Volume 3

HUNTER WRITERS CENTRE

Grieve Volume 3
Hunter Writers Centre
Newcastle NSW 2300

Email: publishing@hunterwriterscentre.org
Website: www.grieveproject.org

Grieve: Stories and Poems about Grief and Loss

22 21 20 19 18   1 2 3 4 5
ISBN-978-0-9954409-9-9 (paperback)

Cover design by HWC Publishing
Typesetting by HWC Publishing
2015 Published by Hunter Writers Centre Inc.

© Each short story/poem is copyright of the respective author
© This collection copyright of Hunter Writers Centre

All rights reserved.
No part of this publication may be reproduced, stored in a retrieval system, or transmitted in any form by any means electronic, mechanical, photocopying, recording or otherwise without the prior consent of the publishers.

Table of Contents

31.1.2015 — 1
Rebecca James

If — 2
Penny Lane

In Your Wake — 4
Anna Lundmark

Losing Elizabeth — 5
Mary Bingham

Don't Think About it — 6
Janet Lee

Invisible — 8
Nicole Rogers

No Questions Asked — 9
Kate Kelsen

Cherub — 10
Michael Tippett

Geiger Arrhythmia — 12
Rafael S. W.

Stargardt's Syndrome — 13
Brett Dionysius

Waiting Beside You — 14
Andy Kissane

A Story About Love — 15
Jenny Pollak

Celebration — 16
Anthony Lawrence

Waiting — 18
Holly Bruce

Gregorian Curse — 19
Afton Fife

Nizar, Little One — 20
Crystal Berry

She is Only Empty Hands   21
Edwina Shaw

Silent Grief   22
Margaret Quon

I Love You. I Hate You.   24
Emma Jarvie

The Art of Losing   25
Jill McKeowen

Surviving Death   26
Hilton Koppe

Empty Space   28
Caroline St George

Waterhen   29
Rosanne Dingli

For My Mother   30
Gail Hennessy

Seven   32
Dan Frauenfelder

A Train for You   34
Finegan Kruckemeyer

Remembrance   35
Malcolm St Hill

Grief is a Mountain   36
Melissa Smith

Love Me Knots   38
Dianne Turner

A Different Grief   40
Siobhan Hewson

Seasons of Falling   41
Techa Beaumont

An Unnoticed Hero   42
Ashlee Pleffer

Animal Crackers   44
Sian Prior

Before, After   46
Renee Bugg

Grief—a View from my Living Room — 48
John Gallop

Upon Approaching a Dead Body in a Hospice — 50
Cameron Semmens

'But your son chose to die . . . mine didn't' — 52
Jacqueline Becker

I Dip Into Pain — 53
Vicki Renner

Eggshells — 54
Meg Dunley

The Impassable Gulf — 56
Jean Pearce

Exploring Grief — 58
Cheryl Hornby

Destruction at the Hands of a Monster — 60
Ashlee Tomlin-Byrne

Jam Donuts — 61
Catherine Krejany

Grief: Companion, Terrorist, Teacher — 62
Linda Harding

Missing Person — 64
Mark Miller

Emotional Amputee — 66
Madison Godfrey

Home Now — 67
Caren Veale

Kicking the Dog — 68
Chris Brophy

Last Words — 70
Amanda Woolnough

Life or Death — 72
Inge Danaher

Lillian — 74
K. M. Ross

Grief Sits with Me — 76
Elise Young

Mamma Spun Magic — 77
Abigail Cini

Might have Been — 78
Ashton von Westmeath

Mother's Day — 80
Vanessa Yenson

Margaret and Ian — 82
Alexandra Wilson

Mourning the Reflection — 83
Anita Bickle

My Way Home — 84
Diana Threlfo

Old Dog — 86
Mary-Ellen Mullane

Remember — 88
Dee Taylor

My Beautiful — 90
Sharyn Williams

Something Like Culture Shock — 91
Elizabeth Timperley

Thawed — 92
Pamela Davies

The Nanny Tree — 94
MaryAnne Grace

The Longest Thread — 95
Mireille Bucher

Noisy Silence — 96
Alicia Bruzzone

The Photo in the Black Frame — 98
Geoff Stickland

The Two-Vertex Triangle — 100
Adela Abu-Arab

These Tears? — 101
Kim Miller

Remembering Alice Mary Nag	102
They Say . . . Janice Butera	104
Three Strikes Sheryl Byfield	105
Time to Go Anne Connor	106
Tiny's House Gayelene Carbis	108
Torn Apart Lydia C. Lee	110
Waiting for the Tears C. L. Fulton	111
Cosmetic Options Megan McGowan	112
Fragile Damen O'Brien	114
The Day I Killed Daisy Leearne Di Michiel	115
Vivienne's Letter Lucinda Ann	116
War with no Winners Samuel Aubin	118
Mourning Bird Judy Hooworth	119
We Remember Too . . . Annika Leslie	120
What's the Score? Anna McCormack	122
Why Don't Women Just Leave? Laura Lee	124

There is no pain so great as the memory of joy in present grief

- Aeschylus

Introduction

Aeschylus lived 400 BCE. He was an Ancient Greek writer of Tragedies and is considered the 'Father of the Tragedy'. It is not surprising that it was he who identified the dichotomy of grief: the pain produced by joyous memories when we are suffering grief.

This anthology contains poems and stories that show the memories of joy alongside the tragic feelings associated with grief. The grief and loss felt from suicide, disability, death and much more are described, reflected on and captured so poignantly in this collection. Grief can be loud or quiet, shared with others or experienced in isolation. Occasionally comforting, often a struggle.

It is hoped this anthology will give you support in your grief and provide you with well written, fresh perspectives on an emotional experience as ancient as the Ancient Greeks, as old as the human condition itself. At the very least, this book is designed to show you that you are not alone and that to grieve is to be human.

Karen Crofts
Director
Hunter Writers Centre
Australia
www.grieveproject.org

31.1.2015

Rebecca James

We walked in circles for nine hours. Our feet covered in earth and our faces stained with tears. My face burnt from the salt. I had never felt the sensation of raw skin from my own tears. We walked and stood. We knelt and leant. There was nothing else to do; there was nothing to say. There was nothing but a garage door between his body and us and there was nothing to do but to walk circles in the earth, on the acres he loved.

His mother offered us tea. His mother. She was his mother and she offered us tea. All she could do was offer us tea and all we could do was stare.

If we had arrived earlier.

If we had but known.

But we did know.

We knew that he felt the dark and that we could not protect him from it.

But we did not know he would do this.

So we crouched in the earth, our eyes glazed, our faces numb.

Hours passed and we said nothing. There were no words. We had no words because there was no language. Just a sick, dry, twisted feeling that turned to numb. That's what the body does when it goes into shock. It stops feeling. When the body can't handle something it stops; it goes numb.

We were not there in our skin.

They came and took his body. They put him in a bag.

All 26 years in a bag and they took him.

And there we were left with our earth stained feet, our faces raw and we had to learn to begin again.

If

Penny Lane

A woman I barely know says she understands what I'm going through; she can imagine the horror of losing a daughter.

'I couldn't go on with life if I lost mine,' she says.

I wish that 'if' was mine.

The woman's 'if' means she cannot understand.

She cannot understand that when my daughter died at 34 from breast cancer, I lost not only her, but I lost all the people she had been. I lost my baby, my toddler, my growing girl, my friend.

The woman cannot understand how grief pierces me in unexpected moments. Maybe I see young women laughing together in a park, infants in their arms; maybe I hear someone calling out 'Mum'; maybe I catch a passing conversational fragment, 'My daughter said to me . . . .'

She cannot understand how I hold two conversations while I talk with her. One is a silent, half-imagined conversation with my daughter.

She cannot understand the searing sadness when I sense my daughter close by, yet, so impossibly far, like a tip-of-the-tongue word that never comes.

She cannot understand the urge to run along a night-lit street or an empty beach or a disappearing bush track, calling, calling, calling my daughter's name to find her and bring her back.

She cannot understand that memories which once were happy now bring tsunamis of sorrow. She cannot understand the confusion of wanting memories and mementos, but not wanting the pain they bring.

She cannot understand that the memory of sitting with my daughter in a hospital waiting room and my daughter's gentle nudge and her 'clever, Mum' when I worked out a crossword clue makes me want to return to that hospital lounge to feel the nudge and hear the 'clever, Mum.' She cannot understand my yearning to walk the hospital's corridors to catch a memory or a molecule of my daughter.

She cannot understand how it felt, each time I opened the spare room wardrobe, to see my daughter's wedding dress ('Will you make my wedding dress, Mum? I want to wear a dress made by you.') She cannot understand how the pain of the dress drove me to throw it in the bin and cover it with muddied garden debris so I didn't give in to the temptation to retrieve it. She cannot understand the pain of hearing the bin emptied into the garbage truck.

Every week the bin empties into the garbage truck.

The woman cannot understand that time doesn't heal, time steals. It takes my daughter further from me. She cannot understand the awfulness of four years of growing away from the sight, the sound, the feel of my daughter. She cannot understand the desperate ache of that relentlessly growing gap between my daughter and now.

The woman with her 'if' cannot understand that this grieving life has to go on. For my grandson, twelve months old when his mother died, and whose glowing-eyed, dimpled smile is heart-piercingly hers.

If only this grief wasn't mine to understand.

In Your Wake
Anna Lundmark

There is a hole in the planet left after you. A bit of the earth is broken forever.

    The hole is right at my front door. I stumble into it all the time. The air is thick with damp decay, manifesting in my lungs, my mouth, my nose, following my bloodstream to every cell in my body. Its shadows blend with my thoughts and cloud my eyes. In there I find the opposite of your embrace.

    My face gets smeared with the bare soil. It makes the tears I cry over you all the more visible, like meandering streams cutting through a barren landscape. The neighbours saw it and offered their help to fill the hole, but the roses they planted died and their efforts sank into the surrounding soil. Now I see them shake their heads at me for not trying harder to fix this eyesore in my garden.

    Of course I've tried to fill the hole. I've tried with all sorts of things. But you don't have to be a mathematician to work out that all the alcohol in the world wouldn't fill it. You don't have to be a doctor to see that no pill is strong enough to shrink it. Once I even pushed someone in there, but the hole is you-shaped and fits no one else.

    Sometimes I hate you for leaving it in such a stupid location, even though I know it's not your fault. I've screamed into it, hoping it would reach you so we could share the load, but the sound just echoed back to me. I've covered it with twigs so no one would see it, but people fell in and thought I'd made a trap.

    I sit on the edge and dangle my feet into it now and then. It makes my toes freezing cold, and I stop when the frostbite works its way towards my heart. Because in my heart you and I are warm and beautiful the way that only we were. In there you laugh at my silly jokes and I feel like the best person in the world for making you laugh. You hold me when I cry, letting me wipe my nose on your favourite shirt when I tell you how messed up it is that you aren't here anymore.

    Recently I put a plank across the hole. A task made heavy by the notion of demeaning what used to be you. I cringe at my own doing, but find myself glancing out the window to see if someone dares to cross it. I see them look down into it and turn back midway. I understand. I do. It's a wobbly plank over a very dark hole. But maybe someday someone will reach my front door, and if they do, they chose the path seeing what's beneath it.

Losing Elizabeth
Mary Bingham

Today I had a call from the young woman who used to be my kind and loving daughter. The special ring tone that I reserve for her calls punches me hard in the middle of my chest. I take a deep breath and press 'accept'. It's what I am trying to do—accept her for who she is now.

'Hi Mum!'

'Hello Darling, how are you today?'

'Fine. Can I borrow your car? I need to pick up my stuff from a friend's place.'

I take a deep breath before I can even bear to answer. 'How about I drive you there, and I can help you pick it up?'

She hangs up.

My car, covered in the scars inflicted the many times I gave in to her tearful or enraged demands, spends another day carrying groceries; not drugs, nor the dealers of these terrible substances that took my Lizzie away and replaced her with this paranoid, angry and permanently damaged girl.

I gently put the phone down, go upstairs to my bedroom and scream into a pillow. I can't bear to hear from her and I can't bear not to.

I remember my first child Alice who died as a baby over thirty years ago. I still grieve for her, but it's bearable now, and there are weeks and sometimes months when she doesn't even enter my thoughts.

It's not the same this time. I'm losing Elizabeth over and over again. Every single day, this strange and scary young woman reminds me that I lost my darling daughter over ten years ago to a terrible addiction. She looks almost the same (apart from the dreadful scars that cover her face from years of ice abuse), but every time I see her there is less and less of the bright, happy girl with the heart a mile wide that was the child Elizabeth.

I have almost stopped blaming myself, but it's hard. We are supposed to protect our children from harm and I didn't do a good enough job.

My daughter, who was going to have a rewarding and lucrative career, a solid and dependable husband and a pack of happy healthy kids, is gone. Countless times I have sat outside the secure unit of the psychiatric ward at the hospital and wept for our loss.

I don't think that I can face another day of this unendurable pain, but I must—I'm her only prospect.

Tomorrow I will start again, trying to help this lost girl build a new life.

Don't Think About it
Janet Lee

They put you in a mass grave.

That's what the nurse said happened to all the babies born dead.

She was distracted when she told me. Tucking in the corner of my bedsheet, making sure the edges were straight.

'Why do you even ask?' she'd said. 'It's dead, what does it matter.'

I said that I wanted to see you.

'No you don't. Besides, it's too late, it's already gone.'

'Where?'

She sighed then. I could see she was considering me a difficult patient.

'They put all the dead babies and chopped off things together in the one big hole,' she said. 'Or sometimes they burn them.'

Then she smoothed the bed clothes and stood to admire her work, hands on her hips.

'Best not to think about it, really.'

But I did think about it.

And for 49 years I have continued to think about it.

Mostly, I hope you were in the mass grave and not burnt. Then other times I hope you were burnt and not buried.

In the mass grave perhaps there were other babies.

Did your souls play together? Did they cuddle you?

I never cuddled you.

You were whisked away from me as soon as you came out.

I never saw you, just your feet as they cut the cord.

They were blue, your feet.

Your father didn't see even that. He wasn't there for the birth. It wasn't done, back then. The husband didn't go in and see all that noise, pain, blood. The husband sat outside and had a smoke and waited until the wife was ready, clean nightie, brushed hair, a little make up. He expected to see his wife sitting up like a Madonna, in a bed with neat sheets tucked in with straight, sharp corners.

And he was supposed to see his wife cradling a baby.

Don't think about it

There were three Madonnas in my ward. The nurses put me in with them so I could forget you quicker; forget I had given birth to a dead child.

Your father came in and I was embarrassed that I had failed. He patted my hand and said, 'Don't think about it.'

How can I not think about it?

I still think about it every day.

I think about you in the dark, never having been held by your mother, your little flesh rotting away until it is just a chicken carcass.

What if you weren't dead? What if the blue feet I saw weren't yours? What if they buried you alive and you choked on the soil.

How can I forget when I don't even know?

All I have of you is my imagination.

And it tortures me.

Invisible
Nicole Rogers

Invisible, that was me. Sporty enough to be left alone during P.E. but not enough to get on the teams, smart enough to hold my own during a test but not enough to be welcome in the science groups. You could walk into my school and not know I was there, I wouldn't be in the photo for sports teams, or the science club. So when given the chance to be seen, I took it. A night out with the girls I wanted to be, I didn't even think, 'but why me?'

I wish I was invisible again. Everyone knew, everyone stared, some openly laughed. Teachers that didn't know my name before stopped to judge me and offer unwelcome advice, and they all questioned. The simple fact is I don't remember what happened; somehow the night is a blank, waking up on the grass in some field, with blank memories and a fuzzy brain. It started slow enough, an upset stomach, a bit of weight gain. By the time I had the courage to see a doctor and talk about it, it was too late. Mum was supportive, but it wasn't support I wanted, I wanted to be invisible. I wanted to curl up in bed and forget. Anger ate at my stomach, I was so stupid, how did I not realise. It was their joke. A game. I was so naive, how did I let this happen?

9 months of people turning away, 9 long months of quick glances and whispers behind hands, 9 months of isolation in a school crowded by people who knew. But mum had a plan. She would be the guardian and me: free to go back to life, set on track for uni, for a career.

But it didn't happen that way. 7 hours and there was no cry of life, just a limp purple body with no name and a lot of blood.

So here I am standing next to a grave. A small body with a name my mother picked. Looking down at the grass, how do you say good bye to something you couldn't love, never wanted, or even acknowledged?

I'm sorry that I hated you so much, sorry that I never wanted you, sorry you would never know this world or make friends or find your own path. Mostly I'm sorry this ever happened, to me, to you. But it did and I can't change that.

My chest tightens and great sobs escape my throat. Standing here I'm grateful to be alone; I know it's silly, but I'm not a pretty crier. I realise it's the first time in a long time that I have let these walls down, releasing everything that I have been holding inside for so long. I sink to the grass and let go of all the hatred, watching it spill out as wet tears. My grief, an apology to the small body that lay somewhere beneath, me a step towards forgiving myself.

No Questions Asked
Kate Kelsen

The day I let my mother go, I cried and cried from the bottom of my heart, and at the top of my lungs. I felt sick to my stomach and short of breath. I had held out for as long as I could. I didn't want to do it. I thought I had finally defeated evil, but in the end evil had won out because my mother needed to survive. It wasn't because she didn't love me, and it wasn't because she was a monster. She was weak, consumed and unable to face the truth about herself and her addiction. She could not have both of us, so she had left me with no choice. The enemy was triumphant, and it was not fair.

A lifetime as mother and daughter had been sacrificed in favour of the bottle. I did not want to let it win, and I felt guilty for abandoning my mother after everything we had survived already. I had given her multiple chances to redeem herself, forgiving her over and over again. I had done all I could do and said all I could say, and I had to realize that right now, she would not be the one to make the change for us. It had to be me, because I was the only person whose actions I could control. I explained that my decision was a response to the one she had made. I had to make up my own mind to let her go, and hope that someday she would come around, having realized what she had lost.

In an instant, all the memories that I had held dear throughout my life with my mother were snatched away from me. Their sudden demotion to worthlessness was just as painful as the separation I was imposing upon us; those treasured remnants that had been my strength, and reminded me of when the times were good, now only served to cause me more grief.

Over time the deep sense of loss I felt after shutting down contact with my mother has turned to anger and bitterness. What was supposed to be a healing process has only plunged me further into hopelessness and misery. I have to stand my ground, but some days I just want to pick up the phone and pour out my forgiveness to her. For all the hatred that has brewed inside of me, I find myself pleading to God to bring my mother back. I cannot live with the hole her absence has left in my life. From a distance I feel her love every day, and I will not give up hope. I know my real mother is in there somewhere, and I pray that someday she will be brave enough to step outside the safety of the bottle. If only she would want another chance, if only she would truly want to help herself, I would give her my forgiveness, no questions asked.

Cherub
Michael Tippett

I used to be a selfish man.

Never cruel or avaricious; merely unaccustomed to living outside myself. That all changed the moment you arrived. There you were, the very best of me, a tiny bundle full of promise and possibilities.

Watching you grow was a delight. Each day delivered a magic show and I was enthralled by even your simplest trick. It's a wondrous thing to witness a human being take shape. To see them thrive and develop a sense of self. Barely three years old and already glimpses of the remarkable woman you would become . . . .

If not for the horror of that day.

Your heart, your precious heart, too great and insuppressible to be contained in a body so delicate. My memory of the events that followed is patchy at best. But I do remember the calls. The animal sounds that roared and howled in my ear as I phoned everyone that ever loved you and broke them.

Now I am become Death, the destroyer of worlds.

Your mother and I left the hospital sometime later, returning to a home haunted by a pervasive absence. The new quiet was deafening.

Your bedroom was now a museum, full of exhibits left to gather dust amongst the fossilised remains of bedtime stories and goodnight kisses and dreams that would never be realised. Outside, our backyard had become a graveyard. Orphaned toys stuck out of the grass like cheap plastic tombstones. In a corner, the sun-faded crypt of a cubby house had been hastily abandoned.

There is a madness that grips the mind when it strives to make sense of the senseless; to incessantly ponder the answer to the great unsolvable riddle. In the end, all I can do is tell myself: *you were never meant for this.*

You were destined to climb mountains.

To cure cancer.

To build rocket ships and fly to the moon.

You were made for greatness.

Or a lifetime of pleasant mediocrity.

Because above all things, you were simply meant to be.

Thirteen months have passed and I still wait for you to twirl out of your room, weaving worlds in your head and inviting me to be a part of them.

There are times when I worry the hurt will never leave. The only thing that scares me more is perhaps one day it will. That somehow the easing of your loss will signify the fading of your memory, and I'll soon forget the details of your perfect cherub face.

Despite the gnawing ache, your mother and I are determined to keep moving with the world. We recently travelled abroad. Remarried in Vegas. I even climbed a mountain. (Plans for a rocket ship are currently underway.)

We both agree on this: *if we cannot live with you, we shall endeavour to live for you.*

Geiger Arrhythmia
Rafael S. W.

There's a crackle of radiation in your bones, this I know
from the times I held my head to your chest like surgery
with my eyelashes, and I heard the clicking. You said
not to worry, but fear had drained you. The ocean floor
makes a similar note, the echolocation of sunken boats
resonating in a ribcage that had weathered its own storms.

After we'd kissed you told me it was contagious, this I knew
when I first met you, and hadn't cared then either. The two
babies you'd never had followed you around, love again
proving to be long term exposure. Some nights you sang them
to sleep. You didn't say what you were doing, but I could guess—
arms rocking. Eyes closed. In both hands, a heaviness.

Sometimes this affair is platonic and we're landlocked in sleep.
The ocean exhales its static, your body rises and falls
like a jumping castle for dead girls. We don't have the words
for this, so instead we kiss. Each night you tell me there's no
cure, that we'll die alone. I nod into your chest, your heart
goes *one two click, one two click*. A blind man walking home.

Stargardt's Syndrome
Brett Dionysius

for Sylvie

She says where our faces used to be
is a great skein of sparkles, as though
the Milky Way's white wisp of cloud
is a rubbing taken from a country night
sky & stencilled onto our lined features.
As though a black hole has formed
where her future used to rest in the
dream job of her distracted globe.
It's as if a wad of fairy floss passes
constantly over her eyes, a childish
prank from which she'll never escape.
She grieves for her driver's licence.
We say that when she is old enough
to drive, that cars will drive themselves
by voice control; we'll all be passengers
of technology then. The young & old
will be one diminished machine, the
analogue tape of our lives will spool
out over the wind-up trees. But for
now, she no longer reads books, they
have blurred into artefacts from some
lost culture, Atlantean perhaps, their
words in a tense pictogram that she can't
decipher. Her bookshelf; an ossuary
for printed matter, her full stops jumbled
together like skulls in a dim crypt. If only
tears could heal the eyes; if only her saboteur
could be flushed from her cells like a speck
of dust, the genes that betrayed her, washed
out. She walks on fault lines, every step
is a miscommunication between her feet
& her brain. New places are haunted houses.
She is only comfortable with routine spaces,
& reacts as though possessed or spell cast.
If ancient Greek, she would have been an
Oracle, the future clouded for all but her.

Waiting Beside You
Andy Kissane

All I can do is sit by your bed and watch you die.
I don't yet know that what I am feeding you
will become your last meal on this earth.

Spoon after spoon of thickened water because
it's easier to swallow and a few spoonfuls
of pumpkin soup, though spoon*ful* is a misnomer.

Your appetite has shrunk along with your body.
Parched lips, eyes firmly shut, your white hair combed
back against the pillow. I watch your mouth slowly opening

as I balance the spoon and tip the clear, wobbling
liquid onto your tongue. Occasionally I miss and mop
your cheek with a tissue. You say, 'Please'

and 'Thank you' as if you have decided to teach
by example, impart the perfect manners that rarely
graced a table crowded with five boys who learnt

to eat quickly or go hungry. When I think of the word *mother*
I see you with an apron on, peeling potatoes, the black pot
simmering on the stove. I think how we took for granted

the steaming plates you placed in front of us, night after night,
how the kitchen was a no-man's-land you patrolled,
how peace was the sound of boys with heads down,

eating heartily. Everything has changed. Now we
can cook: goat curry, fish wrapped in banana leaves,
upside-down plum cake. Recipes are for sharing.

I lift the spoon to your lips and you say, 'Thanks,
I've had enough.' I listen to the rattle in your chest,
how each breath you take seems to fill up the room.

When I think of love I will always see a tablecloth—
knives, forks and spoons in their places, serviettes.
I will always hear your welcome cry, 'Dinner is ready.'

A Story About Love

Jenny Pollak

She's fighting with herself as she leaves his room, trying not to fall apart before she reaches the nurse's station; all along the corridor gathering herself up, as if the foyer was a hurdle she had to leap—every day asking herself the same question: how can she possibly leave him here? And thinking, even as she drives off and rounds the corner and accelerates into the next street, and the street after that, and the following suburb; even as she's parking the car and walking down the public wharf, about turning around and going back.

For eleven years she will fight with herself as she leaves him here. She is thirty eight years old, he is forty four. He needs her to help him reach for his water bottle, she needs him to reach for her hand. Their needs collide helplessly in the air as they pass each other by.

She watches it go, the life they'd planned, made impotent by circumstance, watches it drain away with the urine into the catheter bag, diminishing with every interruption of the nurses and the cleaners and the laundry ladies as they walk in and out of his room; overwhelmed by something caustic in the air.

It's fighting as it goes, this life of theirs, refusing to be diminished in this way, resisting being made to acquiesce to the demands of this tyrannical contraction, dying slowly at being asked to become so much less than they had hoped; full of sadness at being asked to become so much more—their life together, drowning in sorrow, draining away in yellow into the catheter bag.

She doesn't know how to stay and not be diminished, and so she goes; she leaves the nursing home because she does not find him here: not in his room, where another man sits—a man who resembles him, is surely him, who cannot be him—nor in their sad, lost conversation which stumbles over tiny insurmountable obstacles in such stubborn ambition. She leaves because he can no longer see who she is and because she's frightened of losing herself the way that he has become lost. She leaves because she hopes she'll find him again, when she's alone and can search for him in the shadows of their house.

And she fights against her guilt in leaving him, in not finding the right time to leave, knowing she could stay here all day and there would never be a right time; and stays then, for the time it takes to feed him his meal, learning to let go a little more, to let feeding him be her goal.

The time passes simply and slowly, spoon by spoon, one mouthful at a time, and the idea she has of who they are steadily contracts and expands like the walls of a house contracting and expanding in the sun and the shade.

Celebration
Anthony Lawrence

In the months that followed my father's last hurrah,
after his opiate-assisted words about his wish
to be seen as a good father, and also a man
who'd rather play rugby for his state and lose
his teeth than see the dream of being formally

wild slip by, I read through the cards and letters
he'd sent home from Japan, where at twenty
he'd gone to learn about other forms of animal
husbandry and while there, he discovered a love
of sake and fine ceramics, and he'd hold a tea-cup

to the light for me to see the face of a Geisha
embossed in feather-fine porcelain, and often,
when he'd get sentimental, he'd read aloud
from a poet whose name I can't remember
but whose words made a spell around my ideas

of what love might mean, after all I was young,
perhaps nine or ten, and at night, when
he thought I was asleep, I'd steal out to watch him
in his old red chair by the window, tilting
a shot glass to the glow of a reading lamp

and then, as if someone were in attendance,
someone for whom the words were spoken
as if to summon magic from a suburban night,
he'd sip and tell the story of the region, its water,
the whisky a nightly celebration of the history

of Islay or Arran, and after he had been
diagnosed with a quick-release limit to his time,
we bought two bottles of his favourite single malt,
one to drink in the manner he preferred, slowly
and at night, with a running commentary,

the other for after his funeral, and so now,
when alone, and missing him, I open one
of his recommendations, and look to him
by which I mean all points of the compass,
and tell a story, and drink, and say his name.

Waiting
Holly Bruce

Our relationship mimicked our shared blood, cells suspended in liquid; together yet separate. We communicated by osmosis it seemed; thought and feeling washed between us. Bonnets of blonde hair drawn together in childhood conspiracy; I remember knowing you. Our names always said in one breath, mine followed yours. Games with complex secret rules were devised by you and played endlessly by us.

The infancy of our relationship unfurled into hard angles of adolescence; fixed immovable rights and wrongs. Life slammed petitions between us, conflicts and compromises of loyalty. We crouched behind them and waited.

Life's landscape morphed. The small island of origin stretched to new creation and you hid there. Your chosen leader practiced new politics and policy; your line of defence. Borders were guarded, impossible to cross. Were you avoiding me? Or was it you, when faced with the context of me, you avoided?

Our communication staggered; a tentative conversational navigation through the shadow and stain of grudge, hurt, and misunderstanding. It was not our native tongue, yet one we had arrived at; our second language. Silent words and repressed feelings solidified, every meeting a wasteland camouflaged by meaningless chatter. We waited.

Our heads became bottle blonde, a vain artifice of reclamation. We had been awash for decades in a complicated chemistry of event, perception and emotion.

This morning, as first light crawls through grey eucalypts, my hand rests on the closed gate. Iron oxide flakes and flutters from a rusted hinge; the dull glitter of corroded hope.

I kneel to the raw plough of earth. A manic alphabet of words; I need to say them. I know they should have been said when they were soft and succulent, ripe with anger. Shared, given oxygen, they would have ignited certainly, then burnt cleanly away. Instead they remained hidden, hardened, chewing insidiously with toxic torment; a scar of proud flesh towering between us.

Veins of buffalo grass stretch with longing toward outer corners of the cemetery grounds, a fruitless effort to stabilize the shift and collapse of sandy soil.

My words, the concrete corners of them, jam and swell in my throat.

Layers of life lie between us, and still, I wait.

Gregorian Curse

Afton Fife

August 15. September 11. October 21. October 24. October 27. November 14. May 5.

My life is ruled by a complex spider web of dates. The day I saw two lines on a stick. The day I heard your heartbeat. The day I was told it had stopped. The day I left the hospital without you. The day I went back to work and pretended that my life remained in any way the same as it was before you came into it, and into me. The day I was told a tumour had surrounded you. The day you were due.

The deafening silence that greets a mother who never was, is palpable, unintended and offensive all in one. If you had been older, if you had taken a breath, your passing would have been met with flowers, cards and platitudes. But instead—nothing. Fitting perhaps because that is exactly what I was left with when you died. Other deaths are not the same as yours. In other deaths a person does not die inside another. I press on because it is what is expected; and because of the nothingness I am left with, there is nothing else for it.

Eighteen months later and your sister arrives. Vibrant, strong and with so much energy and vigour. While my faith in my physical ability as a mother is restored so too is my confusion about what happened to you. I cannot accept that the same serendipity that has given me this gurgling expression of pink failed you so badly.

As the days progress and your sister grows, challenges and changes I realise that the depth of the loss that I have felt at your passing is the greatest gift that a child can ever give a parent. You have given me no other option but to relish every moment and see the ever elusive silver lining. Without you, each moment of sleep deprivation and confusion over my new role in this world would have been insurmountable. But knowing that I have been given this second chance has made me savour even the shittiest of days. And there have been many.

November 12. December 8. December 21. January 4. August 17.

January 5. January 15. September 7.

March 23. March 25. December 22.

Next week you will be four. I am still staring at the same calendar trying to find a safe date that doesn't conjure up any great hope or confounding loss. But because of you I will keep looking to see if I can find that day.

Nizar, Little One

Crystal Berry

A crumpled afterthought crouched in the rubble
He clings to his son
Nizar, little one.
Memories swirling in the dust motes
The remnants of his house, his street, his country.
The white dust settles upon them
A veil for a father's grief, a shroud for the son.
He inhales the smell of his boy one last time as the warmth leaves him
Nizar, little one.
A father's faith is lost
Underneath the burning Syrian sky.

She is Only Empty Hands

Edwina Shaw

It was seven days before we got Grace's body back from the coroner. We buried her tiny coffin and cried. For weeks I wept as I emptied my engorged breasts in the shower, watching the milk that should have been hers swirl down the drain. Alone in the afternoons, I moaned and held emptiness to my chest longing for her warmth. Her weight in my arms.

I try to be brave and strong. I tell everyone I'm coping, but really I've been afraid, terribly afraid. I hide in the car when I get to the shops, scared of people's pity, frightened of seeing other mothers' babies growing bigger, getting curls, waggling fat feet in prams.

Some people cross the street when they see me, not knowing what to say. Others come and sit and share my tears. Beck, an aboriginal friend, says that in her language they have a special word for women who've lost a child—it means, 'She is only empty hands.' A Greek friend told me women in her community have another baby right away and call the new baby the same name as the child who died. The lady at the Vietnamese grocery says the same thing. She's always asking if I'm pregnant. She knows how much I want it. 'No baby,' I say, patting my flabby belly. 'Just fat.'

Margaret understands. Six years ago her baby lived only a few days. She knows this monster of grief too. She says, 'Gracie's death isn't some mountain you have to climb. It's not something you get to the top of and then over. It's something you learn to walk beside, one step at a time for the rest of your life.'

I know I'm not the only one who has to walk beside this. Other women whisper, 'I lost my baby too.' We hold each other and cry, because this loss, more than any other, feels as if all hope and joy has been stripped from the world; that winter is eternal and spring will never come. We are only empty hands.

Sometimes, when I'm walking along the river, I feel the comfort of all those women who have lost their children reaching out to encircle me, down through time all the way to Demeter. I stretch my arms back up to them. And sometimes, late at night as I lie in bed, I feel Grace's weight, heavy and warm across my chest. She whispers that I will be happy again, new baby or not.

Spring will come. All I have to do is keep on breathing.

Silent Grief
Margaret Quon

You lay slumped across the toilet the first time I thought you had died. A syringe slipped from your hand spilling onto the floor, your pants around your knees. Stirring you in desperation you pushed me away and I cried a deep searing cry in my heart for the little boy I had lost.

Don't touch anything, you yelled. My instinct to clean up, to dress you, to clear away the junk was flaunted by your words. I hung my head, allowing my hair to cover my face as the tears swept silently across my cheeks. Don't touch anything.

Time passed, seasons came and went, your son grew from a baby to a boy, my hair turned grey and with a sigh I thought you had turned a corner.

Captured by your ability to hide I fell into a false sense of security; my boy was safe.

That night, the wind howled and the rain fell sideways across the sky, we laughed as we walked to your room expecting a repartee of quick quips to entertain us. Instead, we found you not breathing, desperate efforts to revive you failed and so began our silent grief.

Should you have died from cancer the world would have embraced us both. An overdose, those words do not pass the lips of those who braved the awkwardness and expressed condolences. Our grief splitting us apart, aching, gripping our throats choking us as we reach for eachother.

My love for you never dampened, you battled a fight impossible to win, few understood even less cared, we both grieved you for the life you would never have while gripped by addiction and me for the son I was losing and eventually lost.

No day passes without thoughts of you running through my head, did I love you enough? Did you know I loved you? My pain would not be so intense, so ripping through my body if I did not love you. I nurtured you and in my heart I continue to nurture you although I can no longer see you or touch you.

I search among your belongings still scattered through the house, searching for evidence you may come back, my madness in grief is palpable, my madness keeps me going for one day I may find you and this chaos of longing for you and missing you may all be an illusion misted by my tears.

My solace comes when you walk through my dreams smiling at me, waving a little boy wave. I hear your voice toying with me, taunting me to follow, for a moment I exalt you are here with me, and then you are gone again.

My longing for you will never cease, my grief will mask my face. I will wring my hands and slump my shoulders sighing deeply forever, my beautiful, blue eyed son.

I Love You. I Hate You.

Emma Jarvie

I hate you.

It hurts, you know, this weight that presses down on me. Relentless. My chest aches; it feels like I have broken ribs sometimes, it hurts so much to breathe. I want to feel your head resting on my chest just one more time; instead I have this unbearable weight of nothing which is so much heavier. I hear laughter from our boys; the screams and taunting that are always a step too far. I resent it. I am crippled by it. I mourn for their loss. I hate them for their ability to forget for a moment that you are no longer here. I hate myself for being so pathetic, so weak when I am needed. But for just a moment in my day I can wallow in my sorrow, be angry at you for not being here and feel so desperately sorry for myself without feeling guilty.

I want you to know that I hate you for not sharing with me while you were still here. Sharing the mundane, the day to day, the rubbish that gets dealt with without a second thought—but does get dealt with. Do you know how hard it is to know where to start? I have no idea what to do until the envelope lands in the letterbox. Do I pay this out of the cheque account? Do I pay it in one payment or spread it out monthly? Who supplies our gas? How the hell am I supposed to deal with all this when most days I feel completely inadequate?

I miss you! I want your rough calloused hand wrapped around mine when I watch TV on the couch. I want to have someone to whinge at about not sweeping up the yard after mowing it. I want that annoying little pile of dirty clothes that lives by the side of the bed back. I crave being looked at with love. I fear I will never know that again and I worry that I will know that again. How do people do this? How do you have someone you have had in your life 24/7 for 15 years, suddenly leave it without any chance to say goodbye?

How can I give the boys the right advice when I'm not you? How do I talk to them about girls? Drugs? Shaving? How can I make up for you not being here? How do I make them understand that the massive ache and wrenching fear that invades them is perfectly normal and will ease, when I don't believe that myself?

I'm exhausted. I want to know that tomorrow I will be able to turn my face to the sun and actually feel the warmth beating down on me, that I will be able to smell newly cut grass somewhere. But mostly I want to wake up tomorrow and not feel the absence of you.

I love you.

M xxx

The Art of Losing

Jill McKeowen

The art of losing is not hard to master . . .
Elizabeth Bishop, 'One Art'

I do not master well this art of losing—
last year our Dad, and now the house is sold.
Instinctively, I grieve for all that's passing.

So many homes we've had—we're used to moving—
yet strange to see Mum taking charge alone.
We pack and sweep, distracted from our losing.

The timber rooms are bared of chairs and laughing,
grandkids, summer sleeping on the floor—
this house of trees and birds is light in passing.

In Dad's shed, we go through shelves disposing—
but linger over tools we watched him hold.
In reverie, we divvy up our losing.

These things are worn, a testament outlasting
our tenured place and days, our crazy hope—
yet will become just things beyond our passing.

From vacant house and yard I turn, embracing
the present need—we have somewhere to go.
The better choice: accept that life is losing—
the art of it is mastered in the passing.

Surviving Death

Hilton Koppe

I am sitting in my father's hospital room.

We gather around his death bed. My younger brother stands and soothes him with calm words, stroking his hair as a father would for a child having difficulty getting to sleep. My father's partner sits opposite, pinching his shoulder and shaking him every time his breathing slows, not yet ready to let him go. Her daughter sits by my side, poking me in the ribs with every pause in his breath. She doesn't know what else to do. And I sit in the corner. Holding everyone. Containing everything. Just as in the rest of my life.

In this moment, I wonder, Who is going to hold me?

I am sitting in the front pew at my father's funeral.

The rabbi's voice drones on in a foreign tongue. I try to glean meaning from these guttural sounds but it's an effort to find salve in this manner. The rabbi nods to me. The eldest son. I stand and step forward. As tradition demands. The rabbi cuts the back of my tie. Something is broken that cannot be fixed. That will never be the same again.

In this moment, I feel cleaved.

I am standing by my father's grave.

Surrounded by faces, some familiar, some strange. The rabbi's voice drones on in a foreign tongue. He nods to me. The eldest son. I step forward. As tradition demands. He passes me the shovel. I brace myself for this moment. Now, I am the head of my family. I need to show strength. I fill the shovel with clods of earth. I toss the earth into the grave. Onto the coffin. With more force than necessary. The sound reverberates in my head. And in my heart.

In this moment, I feel lighter.

I am walking with my family away from my father's grave.

The path is flanked by my father's friends. As tradition demands. Many are faces from my childhood. Some are just names from stories. They usher us away from death. Towards life. Each person offers me their hand. And the ritual greeting, I wish you a long life.

In this moment, I feel held.

I am sitting in the synagogue.

My first attendance since the day of my bar mitzvah more than forty years before. That day, as the time for my reading approached, my father put his arm around me. An offering of encouragement. And a rare moment of meaningful connection. Today the congregation for the evening service is swelled by my father's mourners. The rabbi nods to my brother and me. As tradition demands. We stand. Side by side. Shoulder to shoulder. And flounder our way through the unfamiliar sounds of the prayer for the dead. In unison. A duet for the dead. Uniting me with my people. Across the world. And across the centuries.

In this moment, I feel healed.

Empty Space
Caroline St George

The boy lay next to her when she woke. He smelt of soap and pawpaw cream. His eyes were closed. Soft curls, pink cheeks and hands that had not yet lost the dimples where his knuckles would one day protrude. A part of her wanted to reach out and smooth the blonde ringlets that hung over his forehead, to nuzzle her face into his warm neck but the space inside that now lay empty wouldn't let her.

She rolled onto her back just as Will came into the room.

'Ned called for you,' he said. ' I put him next to you but you didn't wake.' Not an accusation but she heard the frustration in his voice, felt the way he wanted to shake her out of bed, out of her slump as if he thought she could step out of this grief like undressing at night. When she didn't reply, he scooped up the boy and carried him out.

Later when she woke again, they had gone. She stretched herself and moved towards the bathroom but she couldn't find the energy to shower so she slumped back on the bed. It smelt of her sweat and the sheets were yellow where the milk had leaked from her breasts. She felt a flutter within, then smarted that her body could betray her. It was an echo of the child that until last month had grown inside.

She closed the blinds and stood naked in the half light of the bedroom. The mirror reflected a body she didn't quite recognise. Slack skin and a raw scar that cut across her abdomen like a wonky smile. As she dressed she knew that today she had to do something to please him, something that said she wasn't lost and gone for good.

Dinner prepared, she moved into the nursery where the mobile hung forlornly. The sheets, never slept in, were folded back in anticipation. With gentle movements she took each object and packed her sadness into the cardboard box until all that was left was an empty cot. The room seemed to expand like endless space that reached out and out. Then it stopped, shrank, and was just a room. She closed the door behind her knowing that this was more than just closing a door, that it meant something.

At three o'clock the front door opened. She heard the tentative footsteps that came down the hall and she practised a smile. When they came in the room, they both looked at her so expectantly that she felt her heart leap. She would try harder, she told herself.

Ned sat on her lap with his eyelids drooping, his soft curls brushing against her chest. She reached her fingers hesitantly to his face and smoothed away the curls and then nuzzled her face into his warm neck. Inside something fluttered in the empty space.

Waterhen

Rosanne Dingli

Finger on lips, she grasps a lapel, tugs and hauls him
Down a passage awash with light the colour of tourmaline and pearl.
Release comes only after a peck of lips, like a rush of sleet.
Slush, after days of skies laden with liquorice
And washing stained with rust. 'What birds! The legs got me,
Feet webbed and red, look! Black—black and red.
The red of Sicily, mind, not this. See their legs?

Would taste like chicken, yes?' She tries a laugh and fails but smiles.
He attempts to persuade her forlorn face it might be more like
Pheasant or quail, but cannot know, since waterhen is rare
And only seen near swamps.
She repeats, caught on words that suggest a sense of adventure
So different it grinds laughter into lamentation for a distant land.
A moan her sadness translates into: a cry for home.

Wild fowl, they are: wading in backyard muck and weeds;
Squawking full-throated and brave, despite the shock threat
Of humans on a kitchen threshold. The risk of a kill on this
Afternoon of suspicion, of quarrels mended with thawed chicken,
Roasting twine, and pesto made from freshly crushed lemon balm,
Pepper, and lust. Birds peer through eyes of brief hope and extinction.

Where did they fly from, damned fowl no one sees
But denizens of soggy ground peripheral to towns?
Why have they flown so close to towers of glass and mercury,
Aluminium and crystal splashed with caustic rain? She desires to know
And clings to his jacket, damp and darkened from more
Than just this external downpour. Damp with her tears
Wool releases the scent of desolation.

She will leave soon, after these birds pump wings over the city;
A chevron to split the airy dome. She will take flight, in black coat,
Red boots, bound westward, upward. Squelching side-long into a life
Of newly-discovered oldness, on an island of caged birds.
Sitting down to ill-recalled repasts of fowl trussed
And sprigged with alien herbs.

For My Mother
Gail Hennessy

My brother rang me in Bangkok
where I had placed a prayer wheel
on the altar of the golden Buddha

lit incense in that foreign space
hoping for some efficacy
and any gamble worth a try

on the flight back to Sydney
every prayer willed you living
until my return . . .

In the hospital bed
you were so small
you who had been my world.

My brother and I kept watch
talking, singing, telling,
could you hear?

The nurse announced they
would give you a bath
they all love it, she said

I saw you shudder
the tremor travel
through your fingertips

and remembered the story
of the 'aunt' who held you
under in the bath

no, I said, a sponge will be best
for my mother.
It was such a little rescue.

And after you had gone
the terrible sound
that came from me

my friend had warned
the primordial cry of loss

and now all the times since
when I have wanted to tell you
of this, of that, of all . . .

Seven

Dan Frauenfelder

I find myself sitting once again on the back steps of my house. The last time I actually thought about the act of sitting on the back steps was when I was about 7 years old. It was in Orange.

I had just walked home from playing a game of football for the Under 8's. I didn't have to but I kept my boots on all the way home so that the sprigs made that special sound like the big boys did at the games when they walked out of the dressing rooms.

I sat on the back steps, like I did every Saturday morning, and began removing my boots. I felt so mature. For those few hours on a Saturday morning, I was my brothers—I was a grown up. I couldn't want for more.

Mum would eventually come to the kitchen window to do more washing up or cooking or something domestic. 'How many tries this time, Bim Bam?' she would say. 'Three again' I would boast, growing up even more. She called me Bim Bam because she could, because she thought of it and because she only called any of us by our real names when she was angry. Bim Bam was okay by me.

She used to get so excited when I scored tries, more than what seemed natural to me, even at the age of 7. I thought she overdid it, though she genuinely meant it. Every single morsel of her excitement was real; she swam with pride every Saturday morning while I swam with whales.

How could I know at that point that I would never feel euphoria like that again?

Here I sit, same position, back steps, different house, different steps, different life, different boots. This time I hold a cigarette, I'm drinking beer, I rent the house—this time I really am grown up and, of course, it's nothing like it looked. The only beauty in being older is having the price-less ability to think back, to remember times in our lives when things were good. 'Good' like good meant then, in retrospect, not like good means now. Nothing like it.

Another Saturday morning came around. I played my grown up game in my grown up boots making that grown up sound on the concrete and I walked home. I sat on the old back steps with the sun, once again, warming me and began to remove my boots. Everything was the same, same steps, same house, same boots, same amount of tries; one, two, three! Though, this time, I knew how much I didn't want to know. I will never explain but I knew that no-one was going to be at the kitchen window washing up or cooking or asking me how many tries I had scored.

These pages could never soak up how much I wanted, needed her there.

The same heart I used to fill with joy and pride and life every 7 days had stopped for longer than I would ever imagine.

She never goes away, she just never came back.

A Train for You

Finegan Kruckemeyer

A train passes through every town in the world once a week. And even if your town doesn't have tracks, it comes there too. The train is slow and respectful and it doesn't make a lot of noise like other trains. You can't book it and you can't be late even if you try to be. It comes to you and not the other way around.

The train only takes one kind of passenger—it takes the grieving. And it never gets full.

Everyone on the train has lost someone so you don't need to feel awkward when you make eye contact with them. And some might have buried their lovers that morning and some might have lost their mother some years ago. But it's not about that.

It's about the time when the grief is at its most raw – the time when you just need a train.

Once it has pulled up, you step on and find a seat. And then you sit and stare out the window and the train takes off. It stops at other places after yours but you don't have to notice that. Mostly, you just pass through countryside and it's dusk and you notice birds sitting on telephone wires and distant clouds and long grass growing beside the tracks. Sometimes someone chooses a seat across from you and you look up and smile but then both of you look out the window again and it's fine like that.

The night comes, and it feels like a long night, on the train. It doesn't stop at night anymore—it's just a long straight journey without any interruptions. And that part of the ride can feel lonely so sometimes people lean in to each other or put their jacket over you if you look cold but they don't usually talk. They can, if they want to. But usually no one does.

During the night, they serve food but you don't feel hungry.

After the darkness comes the dawn and the countryside looks the same as before the night. You lean your head on the glass and, when you pass a town, you look at the washing hanging out in the backyards or the closed curtains of the upstairs bedrooms. You write a word in the condensation on the glass with your finger and then you rub the word out.

And a bit after sunrise, the train pulls up and it's your stop. Sometimes there's someone there to greet you but often not. You step down onto the platform and run your hands through your hair and rub your cheeks. You move your legs a bit because you've been sitting for a long time and you look back at the train. It's pulling out and you make eye contact with someone who's still inside and wave to them.

And, as the train pulls away, you lower your hand.

Remembrance
Malcolm St Hill

You gave me fishhooks
  for my 8th birthday
You said that you supposed
  that you'd have to give me the $2 now
You wore a black and yellow football beanie
  on your bald head
You showed me a
  Turkish wallet from the war
You told me about
  getting a tick on your privates
    and laughed

You had your blacksmith's forge
  in the paddock next door
Your garden hat was more
  patches than hat

You wrote that there would be nothing of interest
  that you could write to me
You were the old man in
  The Old Man and the Sea

I thanked your God
  for the remembrance of you
You replied that you were
  lucky to have a grandson like me
Your doctor prescribed
  a magnifying glass
You wrote to say
  that you couldn't write anymore
You shook my hand
  like you would never
    let me go

Grief is a Mountain
Melissa Smith

Grief is a mountain where I find myself simultaneously trapped at both the bottom and the top. I stare up from the ground, overwhelmed by its jagged edges and jutted unforgiving peaks, desperate to reach the top. Suddenly I am on that peak, breathing in thick, icy air, staring at ant colonies below me, moving forward without me. The only potential for relief seems to be a fleeting moment, lost to the jump between the two.

My mother and father fell out of love with each other when I was five, and landed with people who I came to love as my own.

My stepfather, Ray, had the leathery hands you would expect of a man who worked his entire life as a tiler. Most of my memories of him centre on those hands; watching them dig through the earth, their roughness contrasting with the vulnerability of the snapdragons he would so lovingly offer to the dirt. I remember those fingers wrapped around a crumbling fibreglass oar as he paddled me in a canoe, in the depth of night, to watch a platypus play in the moonbeam light of our torch.

My stepmother Wendy was one of the smallest women I have met. It was an illusion, of course, a façade hiding the reality of her enormity. Everything inside her was bulging, her soul was a giant and only in the afternoon when the sun hung low would her shadow begin to whisper the truth of her size to the warm pavement. Wendy cared about strangers as though she had felt them kick beneath her skin. She protected me, more fiercely than anyone before her.

They both became swirling water around me. I remained, the stone that shakes but does not shift, fluid with the darkness beneath the stream. Ray lost his life in the night, his car headlights were moonbeams of light as his eyelids became heavy and he veered off the road. Wendy faced cancer, a tiny giant that hollowed her out until her soul became the sky, eclipsing the sun, honest about its size.

Neither of them belonged to me. They were other people's real parents or real brother and sister. I was demanded to not mourn and to not ache; my real parents are still here. I told myself my pain was a delusion. I wished I could believe what everyone else believed, knowing that would hurt less than the truth of love they had both been in my life.

It took time, but one day many years later I realized that you can lose what was never yours. They weren't mine but they were mine, and sometimes two opposing truths co-exist, creating an unfathomable reality.

Often a reality only makes sense to the person it belongs to, not because people are cruel and heartless, just because some people are lucky enough to not have to face the base and peaks of the mountain that is grief. Some people spend their entire lives in the jump.

Love Me Knots
Dianne Turner

You loved that photograph
an unguarded moment captured in a snapshot
my whole life story
for the first time I saw how much I loved you
I knew my love but had never seen the depth of it
and how it softened my face, holding me like a pendant
alone on a string

I can't look at that photograph anymore
like all the other memories it is packed away
stored in the back of garages and in the back of my mind
it scares me to retrieve them

at times a moment flits in and grips me
flashbulbs I cannot share
I catch the emotion and swallow it down
and when I am alone I cry

on that last night
when I saw the real picture of you
the past album of denial disappeared
all memories were frozen
only that terrifying snapshot remains

thoughts of you
still tighten the knot inside
they say pictures fade
as do faces
love thrown away doesn't disintegrate so easily
like autumn leaves it blows around
an accessory to my life
that I walk through one step at a time

one day I will be able to remember the good times
but I will never look upon that photograph
again
you never deserved a look like that
not from me
and I doubt you even grieve its loss
the way I do

A Different Grief
Siobhan Hewson

I have no right to this grief. That is what I've been told over and over again by those of my family who are the most qualified to know. After all I was only two when she died. I have no memory of her face, her voice, the warmth of her hands. There are no lingering memories of regretful goodbyes playing on the fringes of my mind. I don't see her in the crowd and run to her side only to offer tearful and embarrassed apologies to a woman who, on closer inspection, could never be her at all. I don't close my eyes on a flood of images that centre on hospital beds, beeping machines or hands grown cold, with any sense of desperation. I didn't, full of pain, wish it to be over only to feel that I would do anything to have her back again later.

I have no right to this grief.

And, yet, here I stand with a broken heart. A heart in pieces because I have no memory of her face, because I cannot hear her voice or feel the warmth of those hands. My grief is a desolate thing. It is completely barren.

There was no letter left for me telling me of a mother's love that is stronger than the grave; perhaps I was too young for such things. There are no photographs of my firsts: school, boyfriends, dances, graduation, those are the things a mother captures with camera flashes and stores in her heart. There were no angry teenage screams of 'I hate you' to be echoed by her hope that one day I would have a child just like me. And when that day finally came I could not hold her hand and tell her that now I understand just how hard it would have been for her to leave me.

I have no right to your grief, to the sorrow of a lost past, to the memories you hold gently, reverently. My grief is a different kind. I am wounded by all I have never had and it makes me cry on cold and lonely nights and it grows with me through all of life's seasons. I have no right to your grief, but, that's okay, I am already full of mine.

Seasons of Falling
Techa Beaumont

I tried speaking to her gently: 'you have to let go,'
as she grips tight in her hands the crinkled papers on which he was written,
warms herself around cooling embers,
sweet memories of skin,
dances with the ghosts of him
flickering in the shadow.

If she was rational perhaps i could explain away, untie with whys . . .
point to the disconnect:
the holes in floorboards and absence of foundations,
the falling autumn leaves and cool breezes,
the cracks in concrete and broken windows where there should be walls.

But if she was made of this mind,
we would be dry earth and desert,
cracking without clouds or rain, rivers or seas.
Arguing on technicalities we would not hear the call,
we would go hungry for the spaces in between,
too full up for poetry

All then to do is hold her hand,
walk her to the vast salty ocean,
and catch her when she falls.

An Unnoticed Hero

Ashlee Pleffer

Her eyes glisten like diamonds
As she recalls her dreams and the unimaginable.
Her reality that banished her dream
Into a distant
Memory.
Her scars are not visible to the human eye.
For the most part she pulls on her disguise,
A mask to avoid all awkward and painful moments
She has experienced all too often.

But as a person who knows just a small part of her pain,
I see her scars.
I see them in the way she talks,
Even on unrelated topics.
I see them in the way her body sits firmly in her chair,
Something that may go unnoticed to the unscarred eye.
I see them as she sips her tea
With elegance and normality.

Yet normal she is not.
She bears the scars of children who are carried in her heart
Instead of her arms.
She bears the scars of childbirth and pregnancies that others,
Including me, cannot comprehend.
She bears the scars of learning to breathe and survive
After losing who she was
And who she planned to be.

Yet as she sits in front of me
Wearing all her pain as an invisible cape,
I can't help but draw strength.
This is my definition of brave.
This is my definition of a hero.

She did not save people.
Instead, she experienced the opposite.
She lost something.
Something so precious you could not imagine.

Something almost every woman expects to experience
As a rite of passage.
Something she has lost over and over
And over again.
And with it, you could forgive her for losing all hope.
For losing all desire to wake up every single morning.
For losing herself.
But as she makes time to provide me with comfort
She talks about that 'one day' when her baby is in her arms.
She talks about her future
Reshaped by a painful past.

My heart beats faster
Ready to pump out of my chest to embrace her.
Despite experiencing hell,
She continues to dream.
She continues to hope.
She continues to breathe.
And with that,
She continues to shine.

Through her own grief
She has changed me.
She has saved me.
And for that,
A hero she will forever be.

Animal Crackers
Sian Prior

The fish has almost stopped flapping. Its gills are still opening and closing, waiting for the sweet, salty water. Instead, another fish is thrown on top and the leaping dance resumes. Olwen turns from the fisherman's jerking bucket and continues towards the end of the jetty.

Ahead of her a young woman is pushing a flimsy stroller, head down, bony shoulders hunched. She makes no concession to the gaps between planks and the stroller lurches like a toy car. When Olwen reaches the end the young woman is sitting with her legs dangling over the edge, smoking a cigarette. A girl with Shirley Temple curls has escaped the stroller and is poking rhythmically at her mother's back.

Olwen needs to sit down. After the decision last night she'd had trouble sleeping. Her husband had slept right through the morning alarm and right through her last minute packing. For him, everything was resolved. No more trips to the clinic. No more jabbing her in the belly with vials of liquid fertility. No more silent treatment over the years he'd spent deciding about fatherhood. Just the two of them now. After she returns from her holiday. Assuming she returns.

Olwen slumps on a bench and watches from behind her sunglasses.

'Look at that bird, mum, look.'

Silence.

'It's got a leg gone, mum, look. Where's its leg?'

The woman looks away and sucks hard on her cigarette.

'Mum, look, only one leg. Did a shark eat it?'

The woman turns slowly towards her child.

'Go AWAY. NOW.'

Giving up, the girl heads towards a cluster of nervous seagulls. Suddenly she's running and Olwen's leg muscles tense. Just as the girl reaches the jetty's edge the gulls rise as one, circling towards the shore.

'Gone,' she says to no one.

Turning, she notices Olwen and clambers up onto the bench.

'My name's Felicity, what's yours?'

'My name's Olwen.'

'Old One.' The child considers this. 'Are you really old?'

But now she's up and leaning over the railing, peering into the blue broth.

Olwen wants to hang onto the girl's jiggling legs but hesitates. You can't touch other people's children these days. When Felicity's feet lift off the bench Olwen takes hold of her ankles.

'Careful, you might fall. Then the fish would be scared.'

The girl turns and cups Olwen's face with sticky fingers.

'I might see a shark!' she says, smiling a crazy shark smile.

I could just grab her and keep running. Her mother will think she's drowned. She can go back to doing whatever she was doing before this child ruined her life. We'd all live happily ever after.

Olwen breathes out again.

'You better get back to your mother. She'll be missing you.'

'Bye, Old One.' Felicity is still baring her teeth. 'I'm a shark and I'm gonna eat my mum.'

Olwen shoves her tingling fingers under her armpits and turns towards the land. The sea breeze pushes her gently from behind, out of harm's way.

Before, After
Renee Bugg

The stars are highlighted against the ink of the sky, blurring as I speed through the night. Only the road remains constant, anchoring me to the ground. It looms ahead, lit only in the orange puddles thrown from the streetlights above. They flick as I drive; dark, light, dark, light.

The songs on the radio at night are not what is played in the day. The chatter is gone, replaced with the low, lazy hum of an announcer sweet-talking to an empty world.

Arriving at the hospital is a rude shock. The lights are bright here and, while the noise is muted, there's still a sense of urgency, a sense of purpose.

A nurse nods to me as I pass and family meet me at the door. My aunts have arrived from interstate. My mums eyes are wet and red, sore and tired.

We're into day three. Or is it four? They all blur within these walls. A routine of sorts has been established and, like all good routines, we've all found our place, relaxed into our roles. Mine as grandchild, niece, daughter. Mother.

'How is she?' they ask. And it's odd, because it feels like I should be the one asking that question. It takes a moment for me to realise they're talking about my daughter and not my Nan, who is the one lying in front of me, hooked up to the machines.

I stare blankly for a moment before understanding they are expecting an answer. Reaching for the right words to say and not finding anything that could possibly answer it fully.

'She's fine,' I finally manage and take a seat next to the bed. My eyes are already red and sore so I focus on watching Nan breathe; like the rhythm of the streetlights on the road – light, dark, in, out.

The idle chatter returns, barely a whisper above the white noise of the machines. I close my eyes and my mind wanders back down the road I've just driven, to where I've left my only daughter sleeping under the watchful eye of her dad.

Only hours before we were told she has Autism. That's why they asked. It wasn't allergies. It wasn't that we were bad parents. It was an answer after years of worry.

She has Autism and, with those words, the world had shifted on its axis, defined with a clear before and after.

Nan lies with her eyes closed, her skin is papery thin and pulled tight across her face. She doesn't register that I'm there. Her hair, which she has always been so proud of, is wilted like a dying flower.

I reach for her hand but, no matter how hard I hold, she's losing her grip on her future. At the same time we're looking into one that's forever changed.

My eyes close and I grieve for a future that neither of us will know.

Dark, light, in, out, before, after.

Grief—a View from my Living Room

John Gallop

For Myuran and Andrew I keep thinking; how did it come to this? Like a terminal illness their time in this world was estimated but unknown. As the time and circumstance moved ominously on, the legal eagles became more specific with the date. Their lawyers offered some hope against hope of a miracle cure, a legal wonder drug that might arrest the brutality of the Indonesian legal system. Even the Prime Minister and Foreign Minister weighed in—surely they could be saved.

In 2005, when the Bali Nine were arrested the talk was of mules and ringleaders, I recall Myuran's angry reaction and Andrew's despairing look of disbelief as the sentence was read out. I remember not being surprised and thought the others got off lightly. We wanted them to go easy on Schappelle. She wasn't bad. She'd been framed and was too young and sexy to be a drug runner. These angry young men had it coming.

Then it died down for a bit. There was an appeal; they can go on for ages. I reckoned their legal system was dodgy but this was hope. Even the prison governor stuck his neck out and said the two were model prisoners who were having a positive effect on the other inmates.

There were televised interviews (how were they let into prison with cameras?). These guys actually seemed alright. They were humbly repentant and doing some real good, making a difference and having all sorts of people vouch for them. They did not back away from their past. I was starting to like them. Andrew was very honest and funny. Myuran apologised to his mum. They had been in a hell hole for nearly five years with a very dark cloud looming. Surely the appeal would put the death sentence into remission.

Dismissed—I watched on the news.

But there was still hope the story went on in clemency from President Susilo Bambang Yudhoyono. He seemed a genuine guy. He could save them.

Then he lost the election to Joko who vowed to get tough. The illness got aggressive again. The Indonesians seemed pleased.

Another judicial review affirmed the sentence. Myuran's bid for clemency was rejected by Joko before the New Year.

The candlelight vigils brought a mixture of hope tinged with inevitability. Julie Bishop vented her frustration at the Indonesian intransigence. The lawyers hammered away at an unprecedented constitutional challenge.

An Indonesian correspondent stated how the locals supported death sentences for drug dealers but drew back when asked if they trusted their legal system. An execution squad member said he was glad it was not his turn to pull the trigger and would apologise to the prisoners as he secured them to their posts.

The miracle of mercy had evaporated. Only evil remained.

I can't stop thinking of Andrew in his Panthers jersey and Myuran singing as they stare down the firing squad.

Upon Approaching a Dead Body in a Hospice
Cameron Semmens

Stop breathing.
Share their breathlessness.

Picture a beautiful house,
picture this person laughing on the front deck
and fill every room with your sweetest memories.

Walk slowly.
Move slowly.
Anything at speed splinters and blurs.

Watch the curtains.
Listen for whispers.
Be ready for miracles.

If this is a true loved one
place a fresh bouquet of sobs and tears on their chest.

If this is a distant relative, or even a stranger,
a single, long-stemmed sigh will do.

Smile, but don't make jokes.
Cry, but don't wail.

Talk to their face
as if their mind is still there
(it might be).

Talk to their body
as if you hold their identity in your words
(maybe you do).

But remember, whatever happens
is probably okay.

'Cause in this space
group-hugs and weeping uncles
are normal.

On this fence-line between life and death
there's never a comfortable place to sit.

Take a breath.
Keep breathing.
You share the air of their last breath.

'But your son chose to die ... mine didn't'
Jacqueline Becker

In hindsight, that statement was not meant to hurt me. It was said in despair. One grieving parent to another. 'He was a selfish person, only thinking of himself when he took his life, he was a coward . . . .' It does not hurt me anymore.

I have had a lot of time to think about so many things. I read of a young man's eulogy where his suicide was described as a battle fought on his own minefield. Who knew what skirmishes took place in his mind. We will never know. He fought bravely and lost. But did he? Who are we to judge?

It takes a lot of courage for someone to take their own life. I do not want to glorify the act but, to do what he did took enormous courage. My beautiful 16 year old son Brendan, who was too afraid to open up about whatever it was that was troubling him. If only he had spoken to someone about it. I do believe a problem shared is a problem halved. Brendan left no note and I will never know. Would it have made it any better having had a note left behind? I do not need to know anymore. I have accepted it was his choice.

It took me a very long time to reach that decision but in order for me to heal, I had to accept that. It will always be a painful memory. It's not normal for a parent to have to bury their child. It should really be the other way around.

Over the years I have had to overcome many hurdles. One of them was . . . what to do with his ashes? Brendan had spent his formative years with me in sunny California and I wondered if I should take them there, to the places he loved most. I kept his ashes with me for a long time.

Now, looking back, I'm so glad I waited. The headmaster contacted me one day telling me that more children at his school had died and a Garden of Remembrance was being built. Would I be interested in a plaque there for Brendan? What a question. An answer to my prayers. I asked if I could bury his ashes there. I told him I still had his ashes and honestly did not know what I wanted to do . . . until that phone call. No-one needed to know. It was between the two of us.

The following year, when Frankie, my son's Old English sheepdog died, that's where I planted his ashes too. It now has a rose bush planted over the spot. A place that I can go to whenever I visit my homeland.

I am so glad I didn't rush to scatter your ashes, my beautiful, fragile son. Gone forever but never forgotten.

I Dip Into Pain
Vicki Renner

I dip into pain
Like a diver after pearls
Hunting for memories
For the moments that hurt the most
Till my tears
Like an ancient geyser
Force me back to the surface

Eggshells
Meg Dunley

I curl into the middle of my bed wishing to be embraced by the mattress. But the void sinks all around me, beckoning. Every day it pulls at me, ready to absorb me. I'm tethered to a sinking anchor dragging me in. I tell myself just to breathe, breathe, breathe. In. Out. In. Out. My heart slows and my throat opens again. Just enough to survive.

Nothing prepares me for becoming an orphan. I think that having time, knowing Mum is dying, will lessen the dull weight that will inevitably blanket me. At times, I even feel brave tackling Mum's impending death, maybe grown-up for the first time, armed with experience of losing Dad so quickly and the depression that followed. For the first time I'm at the top of my own little family and the thought both thrills and frightens me.

'I'm dying,' Mum declares with an impish grin. 'Everyone can come to my place and celebrate.' I smile, imitating her exuberant mood. The air thickens in the hospital room and I need to push a window open or run downstairs to gasp in the air. My siblings' laughter and jokes meld with Mum's overwhelming optimism. They crowd around her as if she's just had a baby. My jaw muscles ache and wear the pain.

Mum holds court in her blue swivel chair—swinging around to greet her next guest while keeping an eye and an ear on the current one. The room fills with laughter, hot drinks and a constant stream of gourmet treats: pâté, brie and dark chocolate ('Eat anything you want,' the doctor declares. 'Go do all the things you've wanted to.'). But when Mum's back is turned or as I walk guests out, the laughter dissipates. The corners of their eyes drop, rims redden as they open their mouths to say something and instead they give a quick squeeze of my hand or an elongated hug.

My family and I escape to the beach house, the fresh sea breezes. And no matter how many windows I open to the cooling autumn, I can't get enough air. The world is grey and resembles nothing of importance. The skies darken and the garden is in disrepair. I wonder if I'm depressed when I can't get out of bed.

Ribbons of memories flutter around me, twisting and catching each other, some flitter brightly in the breeze, others are dark and sink to the ground. There is so much that I still want to ask her, to tell her. I pick up the phone to leave her a message but instead hear my brother's voice: 'Pattie Morgan has died. Do not leave a message. If you need to, please feel free to contact her children.'

But I have no answers.

We tiptoe through the eggshells and memories scattered throughout Mum's house as we disassemble her life and remind ourselves that our umbrella has gone.

The Impassable Gulf
Jean Pearce

The nurse hoists Mum into the princess chair,
Ties a sprig of heath to her blue jacket,
—A wee piece.

Push, push, push,
Down the corridor,
Closed doors, one, two, three.

In the garden pigeons squat on roof tiles,
Sunshine warm,
Sapphire feathers plump,
Yellow ringed eyes watching us.

Mum's jacket covers her,
Sunk low in her nest,
Arms frail as fledglings, fingers like claws,
Head tilted skyward in anticipation.

Last week she lay down her paintbrush,
Signed her name, a long legged grasshopper,
Under the cherry blossom,
Leaving a smear of vermilion on her pillow.

Once I lay in my basinet under the cherry blossom,
Kicked my legs at people standing high,
Kicked my legs at the blue sky,
Kicked my legs high.

'She's a bonny girl,' my grandfather said.
So long ago, the memory smokes in the telling,
The tree, the basinet and the baby,
Me.

Mum sleeps in her bed,
Our arms stretch around her, half raised in flight,
Attune to the gentle flutter of wings,
The gentle patter of feet down a distant corridor.

I am no longer her child,
My children wait.
My cries rise inchoate from an unknown place, deep inside me,
For the impassable gulf between her and me.

Exploring Grief

Cheryl Hornby

You are young yet what do you know about grief? Thinking about this, I answered:

Over twenty years ago I watched my best friend go through pregnancy only to give birth to a stillborn child. Happy expectation followed by extreme loss. Isn't that grief?

Eight years ago I watched my father-in-law deteriorate as he succumbed to cancer. He used to look at me with eyes that twinkled. He cared, he joked and took me in as his own. He was always there when needed and listened when I was concerned. He found my cat when she was lost and brought home custard tarts just because he knew they were my favourite. When he died I was very upset. The family had lost a creative and caring father. This was my first experience of loss. I thought that was grief.

Two years ago my twenty-year-old cat died in my arms. My family and I cried into her fur as we said our goodbyes. Surely this was grief?

It has not been twelve months since Granddad died. I watched my Nana mourn. I spoke at his funeral through tears that would not stop. I said goodbye and told him I loved him, for he was the greatest man I knew. This must definitely be grief.

Last Friday my son and I were involved in a head on collision. All we could do was pray for a quick end or a good outcome. Luckily for us our prayers were heard and we walked out with whiplash, bloody nose, broken teeth and bruising. The thought that my son could have died made me cry and shake. This was shock, not grief. We had survived a terrible ordeal. After the incident I called my partner, my friends and my mother.

A week has passed. We are healing. The bruises are fading. My teeth have been fixed and my son's nose is on the mend. During this time friends have visited, cried with me and hugged me. They told me they loved me, cooked food and sent flowers. These empathetic souls looked after my children, offered counselling and listened with endless cups of coffee that I didn't make.

Today is Saturday and yet my mother is absent. She has not visited, not hugged me or said she loved me. She has spent no time making sure the dishes are done or there's food in the cupboard. Why have I lost my mother's love? Her needs come first. She walks the earth oblivious to my feelings. My heart is heavy. I cannot be comforted.

I crumple in the corner rocking and howl alone. I am unheard by the person I need most. Now I know nothing more can be done. She has spoken by her absence. Abandonment. It is a soul wrenching darkness. It is not the same as death. It is a pain unequalled. It is self-depreciating. There is no final goodbye and fond memories. This, I realised, is grief.

Destruction at the Hands of a Monster
Ashlee Tomlin-Byrne

I still can't get the taste of you off my tongue; the scent of you off my skin.
I still can't get your guilty off my innocence.

I have cried and as a result I have drowned in shame.
Looking at my soaking wet reflection in a mirror that can only be described as understatedly cracked is the shamed face of a broken figure.

I stare directly back at myself.
I'm covered in bruises and blood where you broke me; stitches and scars from where I tried to heal; all evidence of a monster left behind.
But the tattoo of your attack left across my soul is the hardest of your damage to repair.

I have been a stranger to myself.
Getting used to this person has proven to be a task I was bound to fail.
Trapped in a flickering light, dimmed and darkened by your demon
Your core; your soul.

But I'll bear these scratches and bite marks caused by the inner monster I saw in your eyes that night.
That night you ripped my flesh, bruised my skin, drained my blood and scarred my soul.
I'll wear these scars and bite marks as medals of war.
So only I can see the damage; only I can feel it.
Only I will carry the almost unbearable pain on my shoulders.

Ill surround myself with courage.
I'll live the rest of my life not counting the scratches
Not counting the scars
Not counting the bruises
Not counting the bite marks
But counting the days I survived after being struck down by a monster only I have seen.

Jam Donuts

Catherine Krejany

It is always the smell that gets you. The sinister olfactory sniper that weaves its way along the limbic laneways to the deepest, most buried memories and leaves you betrayed. Jam donuts. Evil things. These three-day-old gelatinous imitations stare back at me forlornly from their tepid bain-marie. But their siren-like scent belies their withered form and I am undone.

Memories flood unbidden. Hot painful flashes, rushing one after the other until a single small cherub-like face peers back at me over the separating months. Time has dimmed none of his breathtaking beauty, my angel. He is perfect. A sea of carefree curls surrounding the widest grin. Round brown eyes agog at the suggestion of a favorite sugary treat. A single front tooth is missing. I shiver at his hot little hand in mine, slightly sweaty, as he urges me toward the food van.

The food-court is no place for a grown woman to sink to her knees in a blubbering mess. Imagined sets of judgmental eyes bore into the back of my neck and somehow strengthen my jelly legs to keep standing. A voice I don't recognize orders coffee. Although I am sure that my lips do not move and my tongue swells and sticks to the roof of my mouth. It takes a while to realise that I have separated again. The shadow me comes forth.

I have come to rely on her, this robotic one. She knows the expected motions, the right angle to hold her mouth into a believable smile, the way to project composure and control. And hope. She can remember to say thank you and even manages polite meaningless conversation with the ever decreasing number of visitors. All the while I shake and sob and rail at pointless platitudes and cosmic unfairness. I can no longer see the little boy at the beach playing carefree in the sand. Only the after remains: the emaciated frame, the gut-wrenching wrecked locks and the ceaseless fluids dripping slowly, a metronome counting the lost hours.

We are not completely separate in our endeavour, her and I. We both understand the utter codependence needed for survival, for sanity. As we resume our bedside vigil she thanks the nurse on our behalf for the TV and the cartoons to break the metronomic atmosphere. I watch the images flicker across the screen and empathise with the descent of the ACME anvil. I, too, am no roadrunner. I am the battered one: thrown off cliffs, bolstered by hope only to be blown up and flattened again and again and again. Yet each time she forces me up, straightens me out and makes us rejoin the illusionary chase. We rise above the anvil and continue on. Because both of us share the one dream: that one day, if we can catch that road-runner, there may once again be donuts.

Grief: Companion, Terrorist, Teacher
Linda Harding

It was a small coffin for so big a life.

At four you were strong and brave; a fearless embracer of days that were to be too few. You rode the slide, you pedalled hard. You loved completely and you hugged fiercely. Those hugs . . . their ardent pressure lingers, even now, in the air around our necks.

In the hours after you left us so suddenly we discovered the brutal reality of grief. How can you feel so many things—and be empty—all at once? Our hearts were shattered. We bled tears. We gave birth to agonizing, gut-wrenching sobs, again and again and again. How can a body endure this process? And yet we did—over and over, day after day.

Grief was a constant companion. We went to bed in its arms and woke there again, sobbing into consciousness, wondering why we cried. Then the horror would crash in like the waves that took your life, robbing us of air and hope. You are gone, gone, never ours again on this earth! And so it went day after day. We endured the endless sweet piercings of photographs, toys you loved, clothing you wore; remnants of a life we no longer had.

We stumbled into walls. We stumbled into people, and their reactions. They sat with us and cried, they mumbled well-intended inadequacies, offered desperate explanations for this tragedy that was ours. They prayed. They tried to help through tender practicalities. Or they stayed away . . . as if disaster and grief might be contagious.

We were despairing, angry, distraught, depressed, numb, we moved so slowly. We had no interest in food or how we looked, or any of the many things that may normally have occupied our minds or hearts. We felt lost, we did not know who we were anymore. Who were we without you?

Time gave us an answer and time changed our grieving. With time the bouts between the sobbing became longer, the sobs less consuming. We did the ordinary things we needed to do: the laundry without your clothes, the shopping without your food, we set the table without your plate, we returned to work. We laughed out loud for the first time, shocked at the insistence of the force of life within us. It bubbled up from depths, unbidden, and with surprising regularity. Without leaving us, grief changed us. And grief changed too, became our teacher. It transformed us.

We finally understood that life is deep . . . and oh, so fragile. We learned that life is precious and precarious; a delicate, wondrous, thing, not to be wasted. We kissed the kisses of those no longer innocent of their mortality. No longer forgetful of these gifts of love and life we were, unexpectedly, grateful.

Grief, that old teacher/terrorist, continues teaching; swooping in suddenly, after all these years, to remind us of our loss and its lessons. And Death, that old thief, waits for us all.

Still, defiantly, we kiss the kisses and embrace the days, as you did, because Spring must come . . . and there is no other way to live.

Missing Person
Mark Miller

1 *The Mother*

Inside her house of grief
it is nearly always
black—

sometimes,
chinks of light
lace the entrance
but the warmth
never penetrates

the walls
are her companions
and the constant tick tick
of the clock from above—

on her bed
she lies like a child,
curled into herself
like a question mark.

2 *The Father*

Shadows cross his face,
one sunken eye is visible
in the slanting light,
white on his cheek and chin.
He is staring out, unsmiling,
at what?
Through the glass his lips move
but no one hears.
What does he say?
He is unmoving,
the shadows creep across the pane
but never leave his face.

3 *The Absence*

This weight of not knowing
drags them down like lead. Like kelp,
like black tarpaulin.

Emotional Amputee
Madison Godfrey

Loss doesn't feel like a metaphor.
Instead, an uncertified medic has arrived
with rusty tools to amputate the limbs you
appreciate, leaving only a fragment
of your former self.

If you lost parts with each passing
funerals would be hobbling affairs
of broken body grief.
Limping lovers approach caskets
on crutches.

When you're internally incomplete
simple tasks become difficult.
Making breakfast with one arm,
you struggle to spread vegemite
on toast.

Loss is not a metaphor,
it is bleeding out from invisible wounds.
Bodily fluids are bandaged
by the regulated repression
of despair.

When I couldn't move from bed
the doctor called it grief. I said I couldn't stand
on hollow legs, or breathe
with absent lungs.

I wish your departure
        manifested physically
so people would recognise this disability,
And when walking down a supermarket aisle
strangers would stop expecting me to smile.

Holding leftovers of loss, I am an emotional amputee
The aftermath of you has severed parts of me.

Home Now

Caren Veale

Home now . . . the feeling inside me is awful—confusing, suffocating. I feel like the world was this horrible, painful, unbearable place. So I found a blanket to cover myself with—the blanket was filthy, smelly and was eating away at me—it was awful to be under—I couldn't stay under it any longer, couldn't breathe, couldn't see anything but its black filth. So I threw it off . . . can see again now but what I see is the same as it always was: horrible, painful, unbearable, black and wasted . . . I don't know what to do . . . I don't want the blanket back. I don't know where to go.

The fear, anxiety, hate, anger, sadness I can feel physically in the top of my throat—like I need to breathe in something that will relax everything.

My headaches are so bad.

I wish I could take something and just sleep sleep sleep sleep.

It's all a game, fake, this day to day pointless crap—conversations, plans—WHAT FOR?

This was written by my sister Tracy Veale a couple of months before she took her own life.

Kicking the Dog
Chris Brophy

I knew my father was dying the day he kicked the dog. The dog was a small King Charles spaniel, devoted to my father. This affection was entirely mutual. The dog was licking fluid oozing from my father's legs, fluid that had first appeared the previous day. I'd seen it. My mother saw it. And the dog smelled it.

My father was in the last stages of liver cancer—at home—sitting on the edge of the bed in his Chesty Bond singlet and now-too-big summer pyjama pants, his thin bare legs dangling in front of him.

'Get away,' growled my father. But the dog kept lapping, the fluid probably salty. 'Get away!' my father said again. And then, the kick. Feeble but shocking.

The kick said, 'I know I am dying.'

The kick said, 'I know I am dying and I don't want to be reminded by this bloody dog.'

The kick said, 'I know I am dying and I am afraid.'

Until this time, my father had been remarkably accepting of his illness. An angry man with an explosive temper, in his last few months he remained uncharacteristically calm, saving his energy for more important matters, his concern less for himself and more for my mother, who had, in her seventies, mysteriously developed epilepsy.

He'd been diagnosed six months earlier. My mother, uncharacteristically calm, phoned me in Melbourne to break the news. After her call, I slid to the floor, weeping. No-one knew how long it might take.

My first trip home after his diagnosis, my father met me at the bus stop, waiting patiently in his old yellow Datsun, his wasted arm resting on the open driver's window, an arm that would no longer build fences, hammer nails or carry heavy loads.

'Good to see you,' he said—and I could tell that he meant it.

Fortunately, even in the last stages, my father's pain was not intense, but day by day, his once-strong body weakened. Neither my mother nor I had nursed someone through cancer. Our feelings of utter helplessness sometimes escalated into semi-hysterical panic.

The day before my father died, I went to visit friends. They could tell how drained I'd become caring for my father. That night, I arrived home to find him distressed, disoriented. My mother brought him his bedtime tablets.

'What do I do with these, Mum?' he asked. 'Do I put them inside or outside?' Later, I woke to find him roaming the house naked. He'd taken off his pyjamas and stood staring, bewildered and helpless.

'What are you doing, Dad?' I asked.

'Is it night or morning?' he said.

Next day, an ambulance arrived to carry my father to hospital, my mother and I riding along up front with the driver. As they wheeled him towards emergency, he looked back at us, both standing by the ambulance, raised his arm high and waved, just as he always did whenever he set off from home without us.

Last Words
Amanda Woolnough

I was writing you a letter when you died. Almost at the moment that I wrote 'Love, Manda', my mobile phone rang. The startling sound of the phone ringing so late at night felt portentous and my scalp prickled a little when I saw it was close to midnight. It was Mum, calling from the daylight of my home on the other side of the world to the dark night of my London bedroom.

'He is gone,' my mother whispered. She swallowed an animal sound of pure anguish. I looked at the letter in my hand. Too late, I thought.

I had been writing to you in my head for weeks. The longer I took to write the letter, the worse I felt. Being so far from home made it even more painful. What do you choose as your last words to a loved one?

Dear Grandpop,
    I'm sorry I can't be there.
    I hope you're feeling better.
    I hope the nurses are taking good care of you.
    I hope they let you out for good behaviour soon.

Between the lines, I wrote:

    I'm sorry you have non-Hodgkin lymphoma.
    I wish I'd taken the time to know you better.
    This is hard to write.
    I don't want you to die.

Mum had hung up quickly. I understood there were others she needed to phone but I longed for the comfort of her voice. I pictured all of the family gathered around your hospital bed, their arms wrapped around each other in those first few razor-sharp moments of sorrow.

I couldn't sit still and yet I couldn't move. I needed to say it. I needed to tell someone. I wanted to lean out of my bedroom window and cry out across the chimney pots and rooftops of Notting Hill, 'He is dead. I loved him and he is dead'. My chest filled with an impotent ache. I had to keep it furled inside me, tight. I decided that this sort of news hurts more in the middle of the night, when the witching hour plucks at fears and regrets, when I couldn't call my family and say 'I've just had terrible news', because they were already there inside the circle of grief, out of my reach. I was outside. Alone. I confess that for a heartbeat I felt sorrier for myself than I did for you.

I could have crept downstairs and woken a sympathetic ear, but in the end I decided I didn't want to hear the words 'great innings', as though you'd been bowled out on a hot day at The Gabba. I carefully folded your letter twice and slipped it inside a cold white envelope. I neatly wrote your name on the front, Mr Charles Swinbourne, and your address across the ocean, in Australia. I licked the glue and sealed it closed, and then slid it between the pages of my journal. My last words to you. Too late, too slow.

Life or Death
Inge Danaher

Sometimes we agree to something without fully understanding the gravity of it. Mum asked me to accept Power of Attorney should she be ever in the position where she could not decide for herself. I had no hesitation in accepting.

Fast forward by 8 years. One night I found myself on my own in New Zealand in a hotel room across the road from one of Christchurch's major hospitals. In the morning I would have to sign some papers allowing the surgeons to operate on my mother and thereby exercise my Power of Attorney. Doesn't sound very dramatic, so why was I in the depth of despair?

Mum had bladder cancer and years of diabetes had also left their mark. I was visiting her to share some highlights from a recent trip to Germany, which she had financially contributed towards. There was a bizarre chain of events. That same night, Mum ended up in hospital for a routine procedure to relieve pain. The next night, still in hospital, she fell and broke her hip, a very nasty break. Due to a gunfight in the city the operating theatres were full and Mum could not be operated on immediately. The immense pain brought on a heart attack, which further damaged and weakened her heart. She was heavily sedated and the operation postponed further.

Mum was not in any state to sign forms or answer questions. It was absolutely horrific to hear her cry when anyone tried to move or touch her. We were told she needed the surgery but that it was unlikely she would survive the operation. I was in utter anguish. I researched into alternatives and found none. Was my signing the surgery consent actually my mother's death warrant? Could I take this on myself? Could I refuse and leave her lying there in pain or have her sedated even more, slowly slipping away? My heart was heavy, I prayed like never before.

The morning came. Amazingly, Mum woke up, giving us a chance to say our goodbyes. She was totally lucid. I explained the situation and she said she had total trust in me and would do whatever was necessary. We hugged and I cried. I told her I would see her in a few hours or in paradise. At that moment the forms arrived. Each time I needed to sign I would ask Mum was she ok with this. She agreed and it felt like all I was doing was holding the pen in her stead. The burden in my heart was lifted. It was a gift from God who knew I could not face that terrible responsibility. Despite Mum surviving the operation, that moment in hospital was our goodbye and I will always be thankful that, sad as it was, we did have that time of farewell. Mum died a few months later but I knew most of my grieving had happened during that terrible night.

Lillian

K. M. Ross

Today we buried my Mum and there's reddish dregs in the bottom of my empty glass. Refilling my glass I recall another death-drenched day.

Lonely, ominous clouds had blighted everything. Fear engulfed me. A bad taste lingered. I wondered if this was how fear tasted. Death was looming nearer. I could sense it. Reluctantly, I went into Lillian's ward.

Lillian gawked. She smiled. 'Hello,' she said.

Hope rose. Did she remember me? Her bony, blue-speckled hand clasped mine.

Dad gasped. 'Mum, do you know her?'

She looked blank. 'No.'

Clearly, Lillian lived in a mangled past amidst a jumbled present and that frightened me. Lucid moments of recent events were scarce. Suddenly, she'd be five and singing nursery rhymes.

'Mum, what do want for your birthday?' Dad asked.

'Fluffy pink slippers and jam sandwiches,' she said, as a male-nurse took her stats. She asked him, 'Bring three beers, love.'

'Ok, love,' he said.

Minutes later, she yelled, 'Where's those beers?'

The nurse laughed. 'Love, where do you think you are?'

She huffed. 'The bowling club!'

Strange, how Lillian had never believed she was old. She'd fret over the leaky roof, insisting she'd have to sell the house to get it fixed. Then everyday items were what-a-call-ems, thingamajigs and she put *Brasso* in the freezer and mistook vinegar for wine. Her hair was once pale blonde, eyes brightly blue, but now she was but faded grey. She'd been strict and didn't babysit but the years mellowed her 'cos Lillian had discovered the club, the pokies and she didn't mind knocking back a beer or two. Although nothing stopped her hassling me about boyfriends and, yet, it was alright to have a drink! And she never caught buses. She couldn't lift her foot to get on so she walked and bragged about helping old ladies across the road.

Dad said. 'That's the blind leading the blind,' and split his sides laughing.

Then she couldn't walk anymore and then Lillian couldn't do anything except to lay in a hospital bed while we awaited the inevitable. Her features too became bloodhound-like with a permanent scowl and droopy mouth. She'd ceaselessly mumble about one past then go onto another. This Lillian wasn't my grandmother, only a shell. A faint smile curled Lillian's bluish lips. I tried deciphering the submerged pleasures playing in whatever was left of her mind but it was merely the torments of the crippling disease devouring the leftovers of her brain.

Then it happened.

Lillian's breaths became shallow, laboured. Death rattles ebbed the remnants of her life-force. Her stick-like hand was warm yet Lillian was gone; she'd left an empty husk behind akin to a slumbering-sprite laid out on crisp white sheets.

Watching death gnawing upon your loved ones is horrible.

Gazing at my boys I wonder if they'd weep for me. But, mostly, I hope I don't put *Brasso* in odd places or think vinegar is wine.'

I raise my glass. 'Cheers, Mum and Lillian.'

Grief Sits with Me

Elise Young

Grief sits with me as I pour the tea. Earl Grey. No sugar. Tiny bit of milk. Don't stir. That's how Mum does it.

I'm out the back. On the couch. Under cover. I've been here a lot lately. It's a beautiful view. Bent fence, *Hills Hoist*, fig tree. Overgrown veggie bed, freewheeling peppermint, slouching chook coop. Old shed, compost bin, back gate. Drooping pomegranate tree, old wooden table full of pots, unknown flowering bush. I've done a wide loop.

There are some things I forgot to mention. It's April 8th. The wind is swirling. The rain comes in quick bursts. It's the post Easter snap. I'm wearing cheap *K-Mart* uggs and three jumpers. I should go inside.

The couch shifts. Grief stands as I sip my tea. He takes a turn around the garden. My fingers twitch. I really want a cigarette. She asked me to stop. He's inspecting the fig tree. They're beyond ripe. The bats have been feasting. We've let them.

I stand. Leave the tea. Step over the coffee table and ease through the sliding door. It's been jammed for months. I'm in the kitchen and the light trickles over the walls. It's 4 pm. Melbourne style. The pots pile up. It's not my turn. I leave them. The sliding door creaks and I know he's following me.

I walk into my room. It's at the front of the house. Mum loves this room. Full of light. Lots of photos. I put them up a long time ago. Before. I blu-tacked them to the walls, the windows, the wardrobe doors. The blu-tack froze. They're stuck. I sit on the edge of my bed. Grief walks in. He peruses the photos. I walk away.

I'm in the living room. There are cups everywhere. Wine glasses, coffee mugs, water jugs. I sit on the edge of the pink couch. Grief sits opposite me. On the edge of the green couch. He picks up a teacup. It's half full. He swirls it around until the tea slops. I look away. Someone will have to clean that. It's not my turn.

My housemates will be home soon. I stand up. Walk to the front door. Pull it open. Step outside. The world is drenched. I leave the fly screen open. He'll follow anyway. I unlock *Norah*. Wheel her off the front porch. Pull my helmet on. Set off down Halpin Street

He stands in front of my handlebars. Just as I reach Sydney Road. The lights are red. He traces one finger down my nose. Reaches my lips. Taps my chin. Mum does that. The lights flick green. I see it all.

She carried me, birthed me, named me, fed me, cradled me, pushed me, kissed me, buttoned me, held me, taught me, washed me, comforted me, brushed me, hugged me, loved me. It's a beautiful view. Where do the daughters without mothers go?

Grief sits with me as I wheel away.

Mamma Spun Magic

Abigail Cini

Mamma's grand piano is the finest instrument you could ever hope to see. It is an antique, brought over from Italy by her grandfather. Mamma spun magic with her fingers across the ivory and ebony keys like the way raindrops sprinkle, so delicately and natural. Now the keys stretch out before me, their clarity muted.

Because of Mamma, piano has always been in my life. Mamma taught me how to sit properly with my back straight and my feet hanging down. At the age of four, I wasn't tall enough to reach the pedals but I learned all about the keys and where middle C was. Mamma would start by placing my finger on the first key and help me meander through the meadow of sharps and flats by tapping out the rhythm. Mamma was always encouraging, even when I struggled to tame the tempo and keep the pace with the lovely, but hard to learn, classical pieces from Mozart, Bach and Chopin. Now at sixteen, I play well because of her.

'*Dal cuore alle chiavi*,' Mamma would say—from the heart to the keys. I would sit beside her and watch her melt into those crescendos of throbbing chords, reaching for octaves, ninths and tenths. The layers unfold and fibres unwind to reveal the heart that beat on the inside. You hand over your feelings to the piano and you suddenly become so vulnerable to the world— strike one note out of key and words may shatter. Then the tempo quickens, *andante* becomes *allegretto*, and suddenly there is hope. When she bowed her head down at the end of the piece that now possessed her whole being, I'd let out the breath that I hadn't realized I had been keeping inside.

I can feel the music stirring within me, straining to come out. My fingers ache to touch those keys. My breathing quickens. Can I play without her? I raise my fingers and curve them a little, just as she taught me. I start to play Chopin's *Etude Number 3*. The piano reverberates as each note joins the sky. It breaks, ebbs, flows, hurts. The notes break through the pores of my skin and into my skeleton to dry out the marrow. My ribs split, waiting for Mamma's warm smile to put them back into place. Suddenly, I don't think that I will ever be okay again.

I wish that I could go back to the few moments before she died and tell her that I loved her. That she was beautiful and wonderful and that I loved her beautiful music and her laugh. But I guess I don't need to because when you truly love someone, you don't need to say it. They already know. But then again when you truly love someone you're never truly okay again. Even if they knew you loved them.

Ti amo tanto, Mamma. I love you so much.

Might have Been
Ashton von Westmeath

Most of you have not had your closest friend shot beside you and then held his hands as he died. Nor I think have you arrived too late to save those in a barred and burning church, but not too late to hear the screams of the dying. You have not walked through the shambles; I use that word in the archaic sense of 'butcher's yard,' of dismembered and rotting people. I cannot ask you to imagine any of this, for, if you can, then you are probably as damaged as I am.

As a child I lived in a city bombed, intermittently, for five years. The top half of the woman who saved and gave her sweet ration to neighboring children lay in the street, her house a hole and a pile of rubble. We were lucky—we only lost half our roof and most of the windows. In the morning, as usual, I was sent to school.

Once the euphoria of war's end had passed, my parents relocated to Poland. My father ostensibly as the third secretary of the British Embassy. I assume that you know that the third secretary is always the MI6 head of station. As the Communists vied with the remnants of the Polish home army, I saw people shot in the streets. I was six and a half years old. Oh, you thought it was all over in 1945?

My first Polish friend was two years older than me, with one foot and part of one hand blown off. He was an orphan living in the four square kilometres of rubble that made up central Warsaw. He stood, leaning on homemade crutches, selling chewing gum given to him by kindly American diplomats.

Later we moved to the country, a kilometre from a small concentration camp on the banks of the Vistula. Originally run by Germans, then taken over by new management. The Russians, pragmatically reasoned—this camp was intended for those the Germans thought to be politically problematic, so it was worth keeping them, and adding a few of their own. While living there the secret police (UB) shot our gardener's brother, leaving his body on the front steps.

Once back in England, under a now thankfully abandoned system, I became a naval officer cadet at thirteen and a half years of age. Indirectly, but seemingly inevitably, this led me ten years later, step by inexorable step, to the horrors of the Mulele and Simba massacres.

Now in old age I wake sweating and shouting orders to men long dead. I do not absolve myself from my complicity in these things. I understand why I keep a fighting knife under my pillow, why, as I drive down peaceful roads, I look for 'pinch points' and possible ambush sites. Nothing can change the past, but when I wake from the nightmares and stop shaking, I grieve, God! You have no idea how much I grieve, for the man I might have been.

Mother's Day
Vanessa Yenson

Some days the truth hits hard—rocking my foundations, crumbling my facade. I put on the mask of happy daughter, playful aunt, content sister, but I know it's a shield—not protecting me from the outside, rather holding in the turmoil.

There were two things I wanted to be when I grew up—a Patient and a Mother. The former appears quite odd, but in my juvenile mind, I did not consider the illness required, just the fact I would see more of my dad. My father was a doctor and our move from South Africa to Australia meant he needed to establish his business. We had brought with us furniture but we could not bring money, so our nightly family prayers were to ask the Lord to 'please let the practice pick up.' One night I added 'and please don't let daddy work too hard,' to which everyone chuckled. I had learnt the prayer by heart, without truly understanding.

The second ambition seems natural for a young girl to want to emulate her mother. By the age of three, I would proudly haul out the vacuum cleaner after dinner and weave under chairs and by the legs of the washer upper and the driers by the sink.

Throughout my childhood, that urge to become a mother never diminished. I harboured it secretly, knowing that my offspring would be prettier, taller and smarter than me. When I looked in the mirror, I saw potential for future generations, not necessarily the lost little girl staring back. In my heart there was never any doubt that I would have children. My faith in that was unshakable.

But you should be careful what you wish for, because although it can take years to eventuate, wishes and prayers sometimes do come true. Dad's surgery picked up so well, it meant he worked harder and longer hours. He would go in early, work through lunch, visit nursing homes and do house-calls at night and on the weekends. Patients would call the house or turn up at the front door.

And then, at twenty, my wish came true. I went into hospital as a patient. Any childish notions of this 'profession' were quickly washed away with the nausea and chemotherapy, the bone marrow biopsies and the stiff hospital sheets. Days blurred into weeks blurred into fevers and visitors and sleepless nights.

'We can collect your eggs,' the doctors said. 'But it will take two months. We were going to start the treatment for your transplant tomorrow, so you have overnight to think about it.'

Overnight to contemplate my Dream versus my Life. I had endured months of chemotherapy and side effects and there was no guarantee I would have viable eggs. Plus I might relapse.

And now it's Mother's Day, eighteen years post-diagnosis. I am happy and grateful to have my mother. I love my family and cherish my nephews and nieces. But beneath my smiles I grieve for the children I will never have.

Margaret and Ian
Alexandra Wilson

Alzheimer's is both fascinating and cruel. The illness allowed tiny glimpses of the man Margaret knew just long enough for her to form something resembling hope, before it cloaked Ian once again in a grey fog that could not be lifted. Even medication after a time was of no use. Ian's brow would often furrow as his eyes slowly blinked, trying to soak up his surroundings. There was a dimness to his world then; it wasn't totally familiar as it had once been. But his goodness still resonated, as did his kindness, and he certainly tried his best.

On some occasions the fog Ian experienced turned to panic. Nothing made sense to him and even Margaret, his loving wife, could not console him. Family became unfamiliar and new places became threatening. A deep level of anxiety would course through his veins and the fear would take shape across the lines in his face. After these incidents, his illness clenched its dirty grip a little tighter around his mind. It would stroke away the memories, lulling him into a state that his academic mind had fought so hard to avoid. All those years of memories and study and hard work were slowly stripped back like paint peeling off a wall, revealing an undercoat of blurred confusion.

Sadness overcame Margaret the day the doctor told her she could no longer look after Ian at home. He needed to be in a place that offered twenty-four hour care. Margaret tried to adjust to being separated from the only man she had ever loved. She thought of Ian constantly, and worried if he ever felt alone, scared and confused without her. She always hoped on her visits that it would be a good day and his mind would be clear. And some were. Ian would smile and tell her how beautiful she was, squeezing her hand and reaching out for a kiss. He loved her and he tried his best. On other days he wouldn't wake for the world and lay sound asleep but Margaret would still visit and sit by his side, chatting about her day as though they each sat with a cup of tea and biscuit in hand.

Nearing his death his words became breathy whispers, like the sound of tiny moth wings tapping against a light bulb. He would try and say, 'I love you,' and his eyes would beg Margaret to understand. His hands, always so cold then, would reach out to her in staggered motions and his lips would form the shape of a kiss. On his final night his two daughters sat with him, watching his laborious breathing as he slept. They knew his time was near. By morning, his eyes only opened when he heard Margaret come into the room and say, 'Lovey, I'm here.' Ian had waited for his wife before he took one last breath, and passed away.

Mourning the Reflection
Anita Bickle

So I see myself as I truly am and I hate it! I am actually physically repelled by what I have become. The myriad of shattered friendships annihilated to reach this baneful state. Incensed at the abandonment of friends and their self-interested protection, against this destructive course that I have steered. That has concluded here, a destitute place, absent of friends or family.

And the shame. The overwhelming suffocation of shame as I see clearly for the first time in a long time, strings of despicable acts. Engulfing shame.

And the mourning of lost innocence never to be reclaimed. The grief that such mental purity can never be retrieved. There is no going back. I have done what I have done. I see myself as I am and I hate it.

I blame friends and family for not liberating me but they have their own battles to fight. Who can blame them for looking out for self? And could they have psychologically reached me or even known how to?

I may bewail and denigrate this harsh soul reflected back to me in the mirror. Lament at what I have become. Grieve the obliterated naiveté. But I have not been blameless. And I own it. I acknowledge my actions and those I have hurt. And . . . and I forgive myself, knowing the dark places that I have been and what I have endured.

In the end, this is my life. And my life to decide what I want to do and what I want to experience. No more will guilt, hate or shame hold sway over me. For in the mirror, the reflection of a survivor stands. This is my life and I shall step up and embrace it. My eyes are those of a battler which can radiate compassion and understanding for the suffering of others. I may live with a dozen shameful memories for the rest of my life, but I will live and they will not define who I am but who I will become. I will live. I will step up and I will take control of my life. I will experience the things that I want to. And I am strong and no addiction will hold sway over my mind or body again. I am a survivor.

My Way Home
Diana Threlfo

All around me people sniffed or swiped at tears. But I stood at my father's graveside with dry eyes and clenched jaw. I met condolences with forced smiles and entered hugs with stiffened shoulders. Just three days later convention drove me back to work where I dragged my blunted spirits through to week's end. Then I tucked my father's frayed blue scarf around my neck, breathed in his Old Spice scent and headed home.

From the centre of town the road stretched ahead, not deviating until it passed the cemetery on the western outskirts. That day I kept my sights fixed on the dividing white lines to avoid the old lichen-pocked tombstones. The cypress pines on the fence-line sighed in the cold wind spiking in from the north.

As I drove the familiar route I listened to the radio; the presenter was interviewing some expert about a breakthrough in coronary care. I jabbed the tuning button and switched stations. Blue is my heart . . . maudlin country music swelled into my black Suzuki. I punched the power off and snaked around a series of bends with only the hum of the engine in my ears. Not far now, just the straight stretch and then the bridge.

Ah, the bridge. I shifted in my seat and sighed. For as long as I could recall the bridge's timber pylons, weathered to a silvery grey, had risen in pairs from the bottom of the river gorge. Each pair held aloft a squared horizontal beam, adzed from seasoned iron-bark long ago. The beams, like the shoulders of strongmen, bore the weight of the girders that spanned the gorge. Recently the planks fixed between the girders had been overlaid with asphalt to smooth out the bumps. And edging both sides of the bridge, like the outspread fingers of protective hands, stood sturdy trusses intent on guiding me safely between home and the outside world.

Something puzzling up ahead interrupted my reverie. I leaned forward, peered through the windscreen. My brain screamed. The puzzle pieces connected. My foot flew to the brake. The car screeched to a halt. It stalled and my stomach lurched. I dared not move, barely breathed. I lowered my forehead onto the steering wheel. Breathe slowly, deeply.

Moments passed in a surreal fog. Then a downward glance through the side window revealed the jagged edge of a precipice. I gasped and swallowed hard. Where were the pylons, the trusses? Beneath my teetering car was a void, a void that plummeted into the river gorge. Nausea slapped at my insides. I clutched my father's scarf and my soul pleaded for my way home to be returned.

Then movement. Outside. A voice.

'Hang on, love.'

Firm hands grasped me, manoeuvred me into the back seat then pulled me from the car. My legs buckled. As I sank to the ground a gust of wind whipped the scarf from me. Somehow I managed to snatch it back.

And hugged it tightly to me.

Old Dog
Mary-Ellen Mullane

He sits there like an old dog guarding his mistress. The other day, when I arrived at the nursing home, he was reading his care plan out loud. Mum is deaf and blind and near death, but it didn't stop him reading to her, almost like a reflex. They have matching walkers; his green, hers red. She is asleep most of the time, these days. But, once upon a time, she was a woman who never rested. I can remember on the fingers of one hand the number of times she slept during the day when I was a child. And so it is a shock to see her in bed, food untouched.

'You should prepare . . .' the doctor says. 'What kind of . . .'
'Funeral?'
'Yes.'
'I look to my father.' He pretends not to hear.
'Um . . .'
'Cremation or burial?'
'Burial? Dad?'
'Burial. Yes. No, cremation.'

Around mum and dad the staff, mostly African or Pilipino, gently do their work. I pat my mother and open the curtains to let her feel the daylight on her face. My own children, and those of my brothers and sisters, come and go like shiny fish in shoals while my father sits there by her bed; rocky outcrop.

'They are both 96,' I tell the doctor. He looks impressed, like they are minor celebrities, or mountaineers or lottery winners.

Dad's clothes are grubby. He is wearing sunglasses, a hat, bedroom slippers. She let him get away with far too much, I can hear my sisters saying.

Mum is propped up on some pillows, breathing through her slack open mouth, chest rattling with each rise and fall. Not long now, the doctor has said. However, time is a relative concept in a life that is almost a century long.

'I can't leave her alone,' dad says when lunchtime comes round and he has to return to his hostel in a different part of the retirement complex.

'I'll stay,' I say. We share the same doggedness gene. 'I'll call you on your mobile if anything happens.' He has a mobile. Dad and technology. He was one of the first people to get a colour TV and a computer. But all of that technology can't change this one fact; his wife of 70 years is dying.

Over the past year, for all of us, him especially, it has been a case of learning to not need her. Having questions not answered, opinions not offered. She has given us that, at least. Time to grieve and let go. I sit by her bed and hold her hand under the blanket. It is dry and cool. Her breathing has slowed. And as I watch her, it stops altogether. It is as simple as that. Through the open curtains I see my father wrestling his walker back along the footpath towards us; at high speed for him. I look at mum and back to him. I can't help but think, she's given him the slip.

Remember
Dee Taylor

The tyres bump the wheel stop and give me a shake. Tightness gathers in the pit of my stomach. Sweat pearls along my top lip. I steel myself and reluctantly slide from the seat closing the car door with a click. The alarm set, I turn towards the front door wondering what this visit will bring.

With heavy tread I enter the large sunny 'Activities Room' and hover. The residents are sprawled into various poses parked randomly in their recliners and wheelchairs. They have been abandoned to the dreams of their youth. Their hair in varying shades of grey, resemble weird cushions scattered around the room in a strange attempt at the latest monochromatic furnishing scheme. The only activity in the Activities Room came from a well-intentioned visitor furiously pumping out a long remembered war tune on the pedals of an old Pianola.

I scan the room. And there she is, over by the far wall. Her snow white hair stands at spiky contrast to the sagging angle of her body as she lies slumped into her wheelchair. I swallow, force my lips into a smile and manoeuvre my way towards her. Her mouth is thrown open with a tiny dribble lingering in the corner of her lips; she is locked in a furious snoring competition with the elderly lady alongside. A precious bag of god-knows-what is propped against her wheel containing, amongst other things, a tissue box poking above the rim, its papery contents fluffed and ready.

Gently I reach for her bony hand. It is icy cold where it has been abandoned above the cover of her knitted woollen blanket of many colours. I give it a gentle squeeze.

'Mum.'

Slowly she stirs. Her head tilts upright. The sunken lips are closed over the false teeth and eyes as sparkly blue as the sky flutter open and look at me. I hold my breath and frozen smile... waiting. Slowly recognition dawns on her and we have made contact. We launch into warm conversation. Her snoring competitor awakes and takes an avid interest. I cradle Mum's hands between my two warm ones and notice how shrunken they have become, the tendons and bones clearly visible, the skin bruised and blotched, fingernails unpolished and unloved.

She breaks into a scratchy cackle, 'You know, there are lots of advantages to growing old.'

Jolted out of my reveille I straighten her blanket, tucking her in like I did with my children long ago.

'And what's that?'

'Well for one thing I don't need to worry about makeup because I can't see clearly enough.'

'Mum why don't you wear your glasses?'

'No . . . no—they make me look too old,' says she who has just turned 88.

After an hour we say our goodbyes. On a cloud of happiness I float towards my car. I throw back my head and laugh at the sky . . . she knows me . . . thank you for today.

Tears fill my eyes, but, I refuse them, blinking them away.

My Beautiful

Sharyn Williams

I loved Saturday mornings. I waited for him to get up. I wasn't allowed to wake him, or annoy him. I waited. Trying not to fidget or get in the way of things . . . Mum.

The smoke from his cigarette swirled up into the streams of morning light, momentarily mesmerising me . . . the ash excruciatingly long. He began strumming.

King of the Road was one of his favourites. His foot tapping to the rhythm. Mum said he looked like Elvis. I didn't know who Elvis was but he was beautiful. He was my beautiful.

I used to watch him shave. He used to yodel. He tried to teach me once. We laughed, my beautiful and me. He loved me then, I think.

I found her in their bedroom. It was cold. She was quietly folding and packing his clothes into that old brown suitcase. 'I'm packing his bags,' she told me. Then she walked over to the wall and delicately grabbed a peeling piece of the blue floral wall paper and ripped it right up to the ceiling. 'And this can bloody go too. I've always hated this colour.'

It was for the best. It was agreed. We would all be better off without *the Bastard*.

I hate Saturdays now.

Something Like Culture Shock
Elizabeth Timperley

I first learned about the phenomenon of culture shock somewhere back in high school. It is basically disorientation when faced with an unfamiliar way of life. I think that must be what I have been feeling, I have never left the country and yet it's like I'm in a whole different world. It is exactly like the world I knew before except it is full of holes. By some freak of science they are invisible, but I know they are there. Sometimes it feels like I am the only one that can see them, but, on rare occasions, I catch other people staring at them too so I know I'm not crazy.

My own home feels unfamiliar to me. I sit at the table for breakfast and stare at the hole on the chair where he used to sit. There is a hole in the air where his voice used to be and my own voice cannot seem to fill it. There are so many holes around my house that it is a wonder I haven't been swallowed whole.

Apparently culture shock comes in four phases: Honeymoon, Frustration, Adjustment and Mastery. I don't recall a honeymoon period, just numbness. I learned many new customs I had no idea existed. There is a lot of hugging. Everyone is very careful not to carelessly offend each other—most people, anyway. The food here is either virtually flavourless or overwhelming.

I do remember frustration. For a time, every day every new person I met spoke the ritual greetings 'I am so sorry . . .' I felt so homesick I almost packed up and left but no matter how far I travel I know I will never be able to get back to the home I remember, so I stay and try to work on step three. Adjustment—getting back into a routine.

I step outside, past the hole where his old Ford used to be parked and drive my car to work. Past the station where he is not filling up with petrol and the shop where he no longer buys lunch. I pull into the carpark at work and relax a little. There are fewer holes here and it starts to feel more normal—at least until lunch time when I chew on tasteless bread while my phone doesn't ring. I start to miss the holes at home and miss my home without holes even more.

I am not sure how you achieve 'Mastery' in a world like this. Maybe one day I will no longer be able to see the holes. It seems impossible that I could get used to them. I've met some who say I will and others who just look at me with sad eyes and say nothing. I keep going. What else can I do? After all, there is no vehicle that could take me back and none that could bring him back to me.

Thawed

Pamela Davies

Sara stared blankly at the unappetising array of supermarket dinners stacked before her.

'What do you want for dinner, Dad?'

Her father, unresponsive, continued to flick mindlessly through the newspaper.

Sara dreaded their ritual. The two of them silently consuming something 'warmed through' in the microwave. It had been the longest ten weeks of her life.

She grabbed two boxes from the freezer and started a small avalanche of displaced items. Amongst them, misty with frost, was a familiar plastic container. She tentatively reached out, her fingers stopping just short of happier times.

Sara retrieved the treasure. Her eyes, drawn to the lid, drank in the comfort of her mother's familiar writing.

'Beef and mushroom stew 3/9/14.'

Leftovers.

Memories engulfed her. Those final days replayed through her head on fast forward. The endless laughter. Shopping for her parents' long anticipated retirement trip. The phone call that had devastated their lives.

Heart attack? Mum? There had to be some mistake . . .

Sympathetic friends and family. The funeral. That dreadful quiet; everyone else returned to their own lives. The descent into an abyss of grief.

For over a month her Dad had barely spoken. In place of conversation, a hollow ache had grown that threatened to consume them both. Without her mother, Sara felt like part of a shattered mirror tentatively holding together but at risk of falling into a million pieces at the slightest jolt.

She hesitated, then stuffed the two boxes back into the freezer. Tipping the frozen stew into a glass bowl, she placed it in the microwave on defrost.

Sara set the table with extra care. Instead of faded placemats, her mother's favourite tablecloth: white with a border of sunny yellow. Silver cutlery. The best china. She adjusted the microwave to reheat and waited nervously.

A tantalising aroma slowly pervaded the house. Sara heard her Dad rise from his lounge chair.

'Just going to wash my hands for dinner.'

Two plates of steaming rich stew held Harry and Sara's gaze for a full minute before they each dipped into paradise. Sara closed her eyes. Succulent and tender beef melted against her tongue and, in that moment of pure bliss, the tears began. Sara became aware of slight pressure on her arm.

'I miss her too.'

Through a mist of tears, Sara gazed at her father now kneeling beside her. He looked a lot older than she remembered. She turned her head and buried it in his shoulder; the pressure valve finally released.

As they hugged, the stew's aroma beckoned them back.

'Better not let this get cold. Your Mum would be cross.'

Sara felt strangely calm at the sudden realisation that her Mum was all around her. In everything she was and everything she did. She scanned the room, her eyes alighting on the battered, hand-written cookbook sitting on the corner shelf.

'Tomorrow night, we'll have chicken and leek pie. One of your favourites.'

Their smiles heralded the beginning of their new normal.

The Nanny Tree

MaryAnne Grace

Toby loved his Nanny. He loved her smell when she snuggled up.

He loved her beautiful silver hair that glinted in the light. He loved her soft wrinkly skin. She always read to him and said 'I love you Toby' when she finished the story.

Toby's Nanny lived just around the corner. He stayed with Nanny every Friday while his mum shopped.

He was so excited when he turned five because now he could walk to Nanny's place on his own, after school on Fridays.

One Friday, when Toby was seven, his mum wasn't there when he got up. She had taken Nanny to hospital. Dad explained that Nanny was ill and that her body was wearing out.

Dad took Toby to the hospital. Nanny was lying in bed with scary tubes in her arm and machines all around her. She didn't smell the same, her skin was dry and her hair didn't shine but she still said, 'I love you Toby,' in a soft whisper.

Toby's Nanny died the next day and Toby raged around the house. He couldn't stop sobbing and shouting, 'I want her back!'

Toby's mum and dad took him to the funeral but Toby raged during the service and had to leave the church with his dad.

Toby's mum and dad tried to console him but Toby raged on for days. He tore up his favourite painting. He tore up his favourite book that Nanny always read to him.

Finally Mum and Dad knew they had to act. They asked Toby what he wanted to do to remember Nanny. Toby wanted something he could smell, something he could stroke, something that glinted in the light. They took him to the nursery and asked him to pick a 'Nanny Tree'.

They dug a hole near Toby's window and planted the 'Nanny Tree' where Toby could see it whenever he wanted. He grew calmer as he went to water it each day and watch it grow. He loved the smell of it, he stroked the wrinkly bark and he marvelled at the way the light glinted on the leaves.

He talked to the 'Nanny Tree' as he nurtured it.

He tied a new ribbon to the tree each year, on Nanny's anniversary.

Toby loved his Nanny, and still does . . .

The Longest Thread
Mireille Bucher

I'm so cold, Ann.

The blue jumper you like, you know the one? It started to come apart at the collar. I keep pulling at the thread and it just makes it worse and I can't seem to find the scissors to cut it off. It's the only one I can find to wear but that's ok. You were so fond of it. Apparently it brought out the colour of my eyes, you said.

I overheard them the other day. They said, well, I believe they said, 'He just hasn't been the same since mum died. He's gone down hill and who knows what he will forget to turn off next.'

Oh, my sweet Ann. I'm still the same. I can still feel you here with me and, yes, I may be forgetting things but no one has been hurt have they? It was that stupid iron! I was ironing the jumper. I just wanted it to look neat, it is looking a little worn. I honestly thought that I had turned the damn thing off.

I'm not leaving here; it's our place, we built it together and raised our family here. No, they can't make me leave and I know you would have stayed. I can still look after myself, I can feed and clean myself. It just takes me a little bit longer, that's all. That woman tried to come here the other day and clean up around here. Well, the place didn't need cleaning up and I told her, I also told her to never come back and while she was there to tell the other bloke to stop bringing food over. The food, my oh my, I wouldn't even feed it to an animal. Bloody revolting cold stew! Not like your cooking, Ann. You always cooked beautiful meals for us, remember the apple pie you liked to bake?

I just wish they would all leave me alone. Even Mrs Bray from next door, you remember her, don't you? I can see her looking over the fence, she doesn't think I can see her but I can. Always interfering, thinking my business is her business!

Ann, they are here now to come and get me. They said it will not be forever, just for a little while to see if I like it and maybe I can make some new friends. New friends? At my age? I don't need any friends because I still have you, Ann, in my heart.

I am so cold.

'Dad? Dad, are you ready? It's time to go.'

Noisy Silence
Alicia Bruzzone

The house was empty when Sarah came home. Devoid of life. Desolate.

Her sister had spent days convincing Sarah she should come over once it was done this morning but Sarah just couldn't do it. She was drained. She didn't want to be with her sister; she wanted to be with her daughter.

But they couldn't be together.

Carla was gone.

There had been tears when she had to say the final goodbye today. They hadn't stopped.

Gumboots still lay strewn by the back door, Sarah having neglected to pick them up. It was as if she kept expecting Carla to race out of her room and pull them on with her five-year-old hands, stomping joyously out the screen and onto the patio.

Today there would be no adventures, no pudgy caterpillars excitedly exclaimed over, no mud pies lovingly baked and presented with great importance. Carla was gone.

The empty hole in Sarah's chest seemed to find a way to grow in the silence, the tightness in her throat forcing her to wheeze as she breathed. No gales of giggling laughter, no tall tales of fantasy fiction and ridiculous riddles.

Nothing.

The silence boomed like a blaring siren as Sarah raced about the house, turning on every television and radio to fill the void.

Noise so she wouldn't feel so alone.

The cacophony buzzed in her skull, like the multitude of voices that had been speaking at her all morning. 'You'll feel better in a few weeks,' they reassured her, warm hands patting Sarah's clammy arms.

The concept of weeks was unfathomable. She was counting minutes. Hours felt like eternity; trapped in purgatory in her barren world. There was nothing left without Carla. She was Sarah's everything, her perfect little girl.

Sarah glanced around the now foreign living room as the theme song to Carla's favourite show blared out the tinny speakers of the television. She didn't even know she'd managed to sluggishly dawdle to the lounge until she found herself stumbling to sit half way through. Sarah wiped the tears from her eyes so she could see the screen, memorizing what her daughter was missing. No more late morning cuddles and chocolate milk bubbles dancing up the plastic tumbler. Just a cold couch where she sat; dazed and disconnected.

It ended without fanfare, no squeals of delight and clapping hands from the usual tiny audience, just a roll of the credits and on with the next show as Sarah stared at the screen. That's what everyone told Sarah she was supposed to do, move on, but she just couldn't. She never wanted to forget her time with Carla.

Sarah smeared her tears on the sleeve of her jacket and glanced anxiously again at the mantle clock.

9:26.

Only three hundred and thirty four more minutes until pick up time, when she could find out if Carla found her first day of school as nerve wracking as she had.

The Photo in the Black Frame
Geoff Stickland

I sat there on the church bench. The funeral of my mother was over. I stared at the vacant stage where her coffin had stood. I felt hollow and lost as I reflected on when I had found her body.

She was clutching a photo of her son Ron who had been shot down and declared missing over Berlin in 1944. We were shattered, mum never recovered. Something inside her died that day. Each year she died a little bit more. She seemed to get smaller as time passed. It was eight years later when upon arriving home from work to our small three bedroom terrace house in Richmond that our next door neighbour knocked on our door.

'Hello Mrs. Simovich, what can I do for you?'

'You had a visitor today. A man in shabby clothes, he looking for you,' she replied.

'Did he leave a name?'

'No, but he need a bath, he smell. Said he would try and come back another time'

'Ok, thanks,' was my response as I slowly closed the door on the outside world.

My mother and I thought nothing of the matter.

'Probably a salesman or peddler of some kind looking for his next meal,' was my response to my mother's enquiry as to who it may have been.

It was several days later when we again had a visit from Mrs. Simovich. A knock at the door interrupted our preparation for dinner.

'Hello Mrs. Simovich, nice to see you again. How can I help?'

'Man was back looking for you. He still smelt and still had shabby clothes. I not like him,' was her firm response.

I raised an eyebrow and stated that I was sorry that she felt this way.

'What did he look like?'

'A bum,' was her retort

My mother walked out from the kitchen with a photo in her hand. A photo in a black frame

'Was it this man?' she asked showing Mrs Simovich the photo.

'Yes, that him'

I turned and grabbed mum as she slumped against the side wall. I helped her to her chair and sat her down. We looked at each other and cried.

My mother sat day in and day out hoping there would be another knock at the door. She stared at men who walked passed in the street, looking for an elusive ghost that was always tantalisingly close.

'Maybe the next stranger; the next man to walk by,' she would say.

She watched and waited, waited until her shoulders had rounded, her head had slumped and her will had dissolved. All that was left were her tears.

'A mother should be there for her children,' she said.

I found her one day collapsed in her chair facing the door. Clutched in her hands was a photo in a black frame.

I rose from the church bench with tears flowing for my lost mother and for my mother's lost son.

The Two-Vertex Triangle
Adela Abu-Arab

The service has finished. Reluctantly you stand up; your sons as well. Slowly they walk to the front together with other men and take hold of the handles. They laboriously carry the coffin out of the hall while their eyes flood with tears. You crawl behind them sobbing, screaming at times. Your sister, on your right, hugs you tight; on the left, your friend holds your arm to help you move forward. I wait a while and blend unnoticed in the river of people flowing out. Like driftwood carried along by the water, I float and reach my car. There's no room for me here; I want to leave.

I arrive home and inspect the place. There are no 35 year-old wedding photos on the walls, no happy family portraits on the mantelpiece, no pictures of doting grandparents with dribbling babies. Nothing. I frantically go to my bedroom and grab the pillow. Clutching onto it, breathing into it, I try to squeeze his last scent out. Nothing. I go to the bathroom and look for hair in the towels, even on the floor, the basin, the bath. Nothing again. I rummage through my drawers and find my mother's letters and some black and white photos of myself with Mum from times long past. But nothing of his. I just can't find him. Hiding for so long in life, it seems he keeps hiding in his death, too. He's become a ghost.

Agitated as I am, I go to the kitchen and make a cup of tea to try and settle down. By now, you'll also be having a cup of tea, I guess, or perhaps a glass of wine at the wake. You'll be celebrating his life, sharing your grief and your memories. I look out the kitchen window expecting to see him; after all, it's Wednesday, 8 pm. I stare at the backyard for a few minutes, refusing to give up, although I know he's not coming tonight. I step out of the house and look at the sky hoping that the moon will shed some light on what's happening. But the moon's been eclipsed; even the Southern Cross has been turned off. I gaze to the horizon then, the locus of hope, future and space. But I see nothing. Nothing again.

Stumbling back to the house, I close the kitchen door behind me, put the cup on the bench, draw the curtains, and I scream. I scream. I scream from the bottom of my heart and at the top of my lungs. I scream and grieve, for the future that will never arrive, the present that has been deleted and the past that never was justly acknowledged. It's all gone. No second chance now. No hope. It's terminal, and I scream. But nobody comes to console me. I'm just the invisible vertex of the love triangle. I'm alone. Just I. Just I . . . and the pain. Forever.

These Tears?
Kim Miller

These tears? These tears that sneak carefully to the eyes, blurring the careful words of the oncologist? She leaves us alone in her office and we look at each other, more deeply now for these careful tears.

These tears? These waiting tears? Waiting in line, waiting for treatment, waiting for results, just waiting. These waiting together tears.

These tears? These bad news phone call tears? Once, twice, more yet, more family to tell, more friends to contact. So much telling through the veil of these phone call tears.

These tears? These across the bed tears? Our son and his wife on one side, me on the other. Between us her unwanted stillness. Her eyes open for that last moment then close. Silent she slips away and silent we share these across the bed tears.

These tears? These final departing tears? An hour of remembering in the company of so much love, then the closing of the hearse. My son and I, head on each other's shoulder, bitter tears shared alone amid so many. The hearse enters the traffic of the city's anonymity but we know each other through these final departing tears.

These tears? These tears at a voice in a crowd or the flash of the familiar red of her favourite dress in the street or the empty house in the evening? These tears of a new citizenship? Yes, these tears.

Remembering Alice
Mary Nag

The church service was strangely cold, devoid of emotion. I wanted to feel emotional, I wanted to cry at my mother's funeral. Instead my mind wandered back to when I was a kid running to the school bus

'You big bold hussy, with your big bold legs!' usually accompanied by a whack with the wooden spoon. Another memory: I'm sick, with glandular fever—mum bringing me eggflips, care and attention. I couldn't be sick forever. There I am, at sixteen, leaving the farm for Sydney, 'If you get into trouble, don't think you can come home again.'

We had a complicated relationship, mum and me.

My mother was always in her own world and everything was seen through the veil of fundamental Catholicism. Outsiders were not to be trusted. The world was full of evil. University was a place you lost your religion. The only thing that mattered—getting to heaven.

Divorced with two young girls by twenty seven, it was not helpful to be told I was going to hell and my girls would grow up to be drug addicts.

It's been two years since Mum lost her battle with cancer. She was difficult and exasperating. She was also beautiful, funny, talented and much more.

I saw mum often, during that time, trying to make up for lost years.

Leaving the church, we started the slow journey to the graveyard. I remembered her words, apologetically, when she was ill;

'This won't go on forever.'

We stood around the grave as the coffin was slowly lowered. I considered her life. A distant relative had explained mum's unknown early life—the violent father, the orphanage, being rescued years later by an elderly aunt and trying to re-connect with her own mother.

As a young woman, Alice immigrated to Australia to further her music career. Marriage and babies interrupted those plans and after I was born, mum suffered what was called, in those days, a mental breakdown. Five children, isolated on a farm, with no professional help, it was a long struggle back to health. This time was rarely mentioned and when it was I would hold my breath, willing her to tell me about herself. Instead she would simply say her faith and her wonderful husband pulled her through.

Mum's faith never wavered and her view on my lack of faith, or where I was headed, didn't weaken. I apologised for the pain and disappointment that I had caused her. Old hurts didn't seem to matter anymore—a loving bond had developed between us that transcended our differences.

I was with mum when she died, it seemed like we were just beginning something that was over all too soon.

As the coffin was lowered into the grave I watched as family members threw flowers and handfuls of soil. Little children, in their Sunday best, running happily, glad to be out of church. I stepped forward, my legs heavy, and threw a handful of soil. Finally, tears.

They Say . . .

Janice Butera

They say you have to let grief seep into your veins to truly integrate the loss. The helplessness of nothingness covers you like a black cloud on a winter's day. Anticipating the rain is like unloading a deluge of tears from one's eyes. The tears flow naturally like the kiss of spring on one's cheeks. Letting them flow is much easier than wearing a mask, but wearing a mask is much easier than to cry in front of you (again).

Grief taps me on the shoulders late at night; she whispers small talk in my ears alluding to happier days when I had you. Grief makes a fool of me on many occasions as we dance a tango of two steps forward, three steps back, three steps forward, four steps back.

Such grief visits me like an unwanted friend. She knocks on my door only to greet me with an overwhelming feeling of sadness and sorrow. Some days I open the window to let her out, it's an intrusion on my happiness. Grief often takes a seat at the dinner table and I politely remind her of the etiquette that is required. Grief is a constant reminder that death is infinite and a passage of rite to all those who walk this earth. In the midst of all this however grief still continues to show me beauty, the colours of dusk, the sound of the waves ebbing and flowing, the laughter of children, the memory of you is never afar.

To fully immerse oneself into feeling the pain of sorrowfulness is allowing and validating one's ownership to grieve. As an act of love, I allow grief to remind me of what I have lost. It's the secondary losses and the empty chair on those special occasions that hint at the reality that life doesn't allow for me to grieve and feel your absence, it begs for me to keep afloat.

As the days turn into months and months turn into years my grief continues to accompany me whilst traveling unfamiliar terrain. I wear heavy boots even in the sunshine but I am always relieved to remove them and let my feet feel the warmth of the sand beneath me every single day, because I still have you and love you.

Grief is my educator, my facilitator, and my teacher. It's the lessons from my grief that enable me to sit and reflect like a mirror to the moon. Some days I ponder how much life has changed since your passing, the reflection I see is a different one. As time prevails the growth around me has been substantial and the days are no longer tinged with so much unhappiness. Your death was an invitation to 'reevaluate' and to 'rebuild' a life worth living because even in death you are still very much part of me, like I am part of you.

Three Strikes

Sheryl Byfield

They say three strikes and you're out.

Strike one: A swallowed coin, 2 years old, your breathing stopped, blueness around lips and a trip to emergency.

Strike two: Hit by a train, 21 years old, dragged along, it made a great story, and all you lost was the little finger on your left hand. You became invincible.

Strike three: You died, 27 years old. An accident of excess, perhaps.

I got the late night knock, the two young policemen, the disbelief, the terror, the sugary tea, the clichés, as the old me died along with you.

Etched in my mind is the last time I saw you, standing tall, proud and beautiful in the hat I bought the day before, for your birthday. In forty eight hours the image had changed to you in your last hours, stretched on the floor, alone, I wanted it to be me.

I always thought I'd know if my child was dying. I will always feel guilty because I didn't. The horrors of my thoughts are always here.

So many changes in so few days. Packing, what to keep (everything), what to throw (nothing). Your funeral, a blur (maybe one day I will watch the video, like reruns of family celebrations). Your fundraiser, to make the album you never did (such generosity from your wonderful friends), to leave a legacy of song.

Then the stillness, the living without you, the crying, the wishing, the bargaining, the need to be shut away from everything. A pill to take the edge off, a pill to help with sleep. The remembering of words, of smiles, of looks, of skin, of living, of what might have been.

I always knew you would have been the best dad. You would have fished and sang and taught them to love and care for the world and all that's in it. I lost all that you were to become.

Back to work, eventually, the feeling of normalcy but life was anything but that way. People, kind and sympathetic, but there is a time limit imposed by the outside, then their focus shifts. Some are scared, knowing a mother who has had her worst nightmare actualised, they keep their distance in case death is contagious and their child could be next.

I left your ashes for a while, couldn't fathom the then and now. Once collected (surprised at the weight, cradled in my arms, neatly wrapped), I brought you home, just like I did 27 years before.

Time to Go
Anne Connor

Twenty years after my father's death, I found out he was involved in a tragic shooting incident while serving in the Second World War. During a basic drill, his gun accidently fired killing his friend Joe Forrester in the back of the head. Joe was twenty-two.

There has always been conjecture as to whether the fatality was caused by Dad failing to secure the safety switch or whether a bullet became lodged in the barrel and sudden movement caused it to fire. Veterans told me the make of his gun had a reputation for shooting by mistake. Whatever the reason, my father had a nervous breakdown and was discharged from the Army, medically unfit. There is no doubt he lived with guilt and grief on his return to civilian life.

In an attempt to find the truth, I set out on a journey to research and chronicle his story. During the writing, I had a recurring, haunting dream.

My father was dying and sitting up in his hospital bed supported by fat pillows. He wore his own green and blue striped pyjamas. The ones he used to wear at home when he ate his breakfast or walked to the front gate of a morning to pick up *The Sun* from the cylinder on top of the letterbox.

The top button of his pyjama top was undone exposing three round holes in his chest from where the doctors drilled for bone marrow to check his leukemic cells. The holes resembled bullet wounds, with darkened blood caked around the edge of each crater. My father's eyes were sunken; his face had a grey tinge and was bloated from cortisone injections. Lank white hair barely hiding his scalp replaced his once thick curly black mop.

In the dream, twenty-two-year-old Joe Forrester walked into my father's hospital room. The visitor wore his Army shirt and shorts. Youthful, tanned and lean, he had a bloodied bandage around his head and stood at the foot of Dad's bed. My father looked up and squinted. The late afternoon sun behind Joe made it difficult to make out who he was.

'Gidday Eric, it's me, Joe.'

'Who?'

'Joe, Joe Forrester.'

He walked over to Dad and sat on the chair by the bed. He leaned over and placed his hand on my father's arm. He waited while Dad studied his face.

'I know you thought the shooting was your fault,' Joe said. 'But it was my time to go. I'm sorry you carried the burden for so long.'

Dad began to cry. Quietly at first then his weeping became stronger. Joe moved onto the bed and sat next to him. My father's body, by now, was wracked with sobs. Joe put his arm around him. The older man buried his head in the younger man's chest and cried—for a long time.

Tiny's House
Gayelene Carbis

We called my grandfather Tiny. Because he was so big, of course, but it wasn't just that. It was his presence, not big and booming, but large in the sense that he seemed bigger than the small things so many grown-ups seemed to worry about.

Tiny was my grandfather and lived alone on a tea farm in East Africa. Well, not really alone—my aunt lived in a cottage on the same farm and there was Mwangi who looked after him. Cooked for him, bathed him. Mwangi had always been there. In fact, he was probably nearly as old as my grandfather!

When grandpa was dying, our family flew from all corners to be with him: Australia, England, Canada. One day he'd woken up and said he was tired and ready to go. And everyone knew he would because he'd said so.

Grandpa hated all the fuss that went with funerals. Not that he didn't want the occasion marked, he just didn't see the point in spending money on flowers or coffins when he had everything around him that could be used for his funeral.

He had his coffin knocked up by one of the farm hands, who'd had no training but was good with wood.

A few weeks before he took to his bed, he walked with my aunt around his garden to show her the path he wanted his coffin to take. It was a beautiful English garden that he and my grandmother had created when they'd first come out from England.

Then grandpa took a shovel and stuck it in the ground to mark the place where he wanted to lie.

He said it was the most useful bit of gardening he'd ever done.

On the last day, we all stood around his bed. And listened as his breathing became slower . . . and slower . . . till finally—it stopped.

He looked like he was sleeping.

We stayed there, quietly, for a little while, not saying anything.

It all seemed so natural and I wondered why so many people were afraid of it.

My grandfather wasn't and neither was I.

It took six men to carry that wooden box with grandpa inside. They could barely carry him he was so heavy. It became almost comic as they tried to maneuvre their way through this pretty English garden with its twists and turns and intricate little paths between beds of roses and under hanging vines.

He didn't want a tombstone, he was simply put into the ground.

There's a mound there now, covered in his favourite flowers—white lilies.

Grandpa's house had a musty smell in those last few years, the smell of growing old. But after he died, one of my Uncles moved in with his five children and suddenly, the next time we were there, there were painted rooms and new carpets and toys everywhere, bikes and roller-blades, matchbox cars and kewpie dolls . . . .

And I thought: that's Africa for you. It just goes on and on.

Torn Apart
Lydia C. Lee

I get angry when I see someone who has thrown their life away on the news. Why wasn't it them instead?

I get annoyed with friends who don't appreciate their husband. Don't you know how lucky you are? I think to myself, but never say.

It breaks my heart when I watch other dads kindly take my son to the Father & Son events or even just the footy.

I feel robbed. My kids were robbed.

Then I feel guilty. I wasn't robbed. He was robbed. That cruel fate took him from us much too soon. Stole all the potential and future joy, all the dreams that would never be fulfilled.

There is so much of him entwined in my memories, my habits, my life. I still make jokes that no one else laughs at. I can't be bothered explaining the inside joke to people when they look puzzled. There's no joke now that there's no inside. No our. No we. No us.

I try to remind the kids of all the wonderful times, of what a great dad he was and how much he loved them. I can see the memories fading for them. Sometimes it terrifies me, sometimes I get jealous. Maybe the pain will lessen eventually.

Maybe not.

His mother, who I never much cared for, is now my best friend. We share our grief. We never tire of the reminiscing. She doesn't tell me 'You need to move on.'

I don't need to move on. I need him to come back.

I need to tell him all that he meant to me.

I need him to know.

A light went out and a world was torn apart.

My world.

Waiting for the Tears

C. L. Fulton

Grief is supposed to make you cry. I was still waiting for the tears. He died last night, so I was informed. The funeral is Wednesday, an eleven a.m. service, with a reception to be held after and food furnished for the wake. There'll be those brown and white sandwiches with the crusts cut off, assorted cakes and pastries—probably muffins—and a mixed batch of hors d'oeuvres (or *horses' doovers* as Kailey calls them). Will she eat them at her father's funeral? Or will she stuff her mouth with her fist and choke back her heartache? Where is mine, I wonder for the nineteenth time.

It was cancer of the anus that killed him. An agonizing twelve month death sentence. Shouldn't have called him a pain in the arse, I guess. When I think back to the last time we spoke, the night before he died, I can't remember our last conversation. I can't even remember the words we said. I mean, what do you say to your ex-husband on his death bed when you've a great rock stuck in your throat? *I'm sorry things didn't work out. I promise I'll take care of the kids. They'll miss you. I'm so sorry* . . . I'm as numb as a frozen chook; off with my head, pull out the giblets and pluck me raw.

I worry for Natty, at fifteen a boy needs a father but he seems quite together. Perhaps it hasn't hit him yet. Perhaps there will be a grief punch at each of the milestones he will reach: a stab of sorrow at graduation, a twinge of yearning at his 21st, a pang of anguish at the birth of his first child.

Kailey I ache for. Pearls of sorrow forge new pathways down her silent cheeks. She resolutely shuts her bedroom door, holding her grief close in the cave of her room. She wears it like a padded suit, a Michelin Man protective weapon. Making a scrapbook from photos and bits of belongings, she'll add to it over time, begun at age twelve when her daddy died. She'll slide her hands across the glossy paper when the need to remember him takes hold. Her heart will pinch and her eyes hurt.

And now I can't remember why I was angry with him. I seem to have left my rage behind with the contemplation of those crustless sandwiches. They lodge in my throat somewhere between guilt and fear. *He's gone. He's really gone.* I clasp my stomach, suck in my breath, dissolve the blockage. The tears make a cameo appearance, fashionably late, burning the corners of my heavy eyes. *It was good that we were friends, at the end.* The dam breaks at last and I sob for what once was and for what will never be.

Cosmetic Options
Megan McGowan

The surgeon poked my tummy.

'We could get a great result,' she said. She looked to my husband. 'They'll be soft. They'll be warm. They'll feel like the real thing.' She turned back to me. 'Of course you won't be able to feel anything. We can reconnect the blood supply but not the nerves.'

I wanted to know how long it would take to recover. In particular, I wanted to know the comparison between having reconstruction and not having reconstruction. The cancer surgeon had said six months or six weeks.

'Well, some of my alpha patients are back abseiling inside three months.' My husband asked if the abseiling was compulsory.

She wanted to book me in for the following Friday—eleven hours to remove my breasts, cut my tummy away and then move it to my chest. She explained how the skin would be pulled down 'like a Holland blind,' and how she'd cut a new hole to bring my belly button through.

She showed me photos of successful reconstructions and explained that my radiation treatment meant I was unsuitable for implants. I looked at the elliptical scars around each of the reconstructed mounds and the long slashes from one hip to another. I winced at the strange, puckered belly buttons.

It was two days since I'd been told the cancer was back and invasive. I'd had chemotherapy and breast conserving surgery and radiation and the best medical team that money could buy. Twelve months later my routine scans showed calcification. Probably just dead cells, said the surgeon, or at the very worst, something in situ. Best to just cut it out. Take another slice.

The pathology said invasive cancer. The multi-disciplinary team unanimously recommended mastectomy.

I told the cosmetic surgeon I wanted time to think about it.

'Well why wouldn't you want reconstruction?' she asked me. Maybe I didn't like the idea of rearranging bits of my body. I said, 'I'm not sure that I wouldn't rather just be flat chested.'

She frowned. 'So you'd rather be a martyr?'

Did she realise that martyrs die for a cause?

I was supposed to be pleased that a top surgeon was offering me reconstruction. My uncertainty offended her. She didn't understand. If I couldn't have my breasts I didn't want imitation breasts. I wanted to grieve. I didn't want to pretend it had never happened.

My husband said, 'Whatever you decide, you have my support,' and 'You are not your breasts.' I told him I didn't want the reconstruction. He was happy and relieved. He wanted me to have the least amount of surgery.

On the day of the surgery I asked if he wanted to kiss them goodbye. 'No,' he said, 'they tried to kill you and I'm over them.' I'll always love him for that.

Sometimes my husband runs his hand over my scars and my unaltered tummy.

'I love you,' he says.

'I know,' I reply.

It helps.

Fragile

Damen O'Brien

It was just a dream, darling, go to sleep—
storms trouble and ripple through the deep.
I heard a Koel cry once, a bat shriek—
the wind shuffles in the endings of the week.
I've dreamt terrible things-a burning wind
tastes the curtains; smoke and tamarinds.
I saw the two of us flicker, the time rewind,
as though a stitch was unpicked from our minds.
I saw our love erased with a key-stroke,
and there was no great change. We were smoke
spread thinly to the wind; a bat's despair—
so easily the world can tear.

The Day I Killed Daisy

Leearne Di Michiel

Since I was small enough to fit inside a laundry basket I've held a secret. The memory is not always there—the dreadful ones seem to lock themselves away in deep places. It comes to me without warning like a menopausal hot flush, the memory envelopes me, holds me captive and then slips away.

I am standing in the doorway. My eyes travel beyond the kitchen: past the red laminex table and chairs, past the vase of brightly coloured plastic flowers, along the lino floor and over the blue rocking chair to the bed at the end of the room. Lying with pillows plumped at her back is Daisy, my great-grandmother. I call her Grandma. Daisy is dying.

Grandma's room feels different—there will be no little bundles of dried fruit wrapped in wax proof paper for me today. I see the silent piano but in my head I can still hear the music: her fragile, translucent hands that could sing and dance on ivory keys; the empty rocking chair where my brother and I enjoyed front row concert seating. Now the room lies silent, just like Daisy. Her fingers gently strum the sleeve of her flannelette nightie; a mohair blanket shrouds her bed in soft, wispy tones of lavender and grey.

At the doorway I stand between my grandmother and my mother. My grandmother is wearing an apron tied about her waist—I remember her always in an apron. My mother is heavily pregnant.

Daisy announces she is feeling much better today. I hear myself saying, 'Hurray, Grandma's not going to die!' My whole body responds to this wonderful news: my little fists clench as my arms rise above my head and punch the air. I didn't know I was not to use the 'D' word. The effect of my words had the impact of a gunshot. I heard the gasps beside me, deep sudden inhales of breath and a groan from the bed. What had I done? In my horror I fled the crime scene and hid myself inside the laundry basket, pulling the wicker dome over me, creating my own tiny prison. Coiled on the grass in the basket at the base of our Hills Hoist I eventually fell asleep. I remember my mother gently scooping me up and carrying me inside.

People think little ones don't remember but they do. Grief nurtures the young and grows old with them. I was too afraid to speak of it. Silence kept the memory alive. I wondered if we were all holding the same secret? It's with me even now after all these years, the day I killed Daisy.

Vivienne's Letter
Lucinda Ann

She read the letter again. How many times was inconceivable now, the fold lines permanently creased in the paper. She could almost recite it word for word. They were as clear in her memory as the brown haired boy that wrote them. But she loved to see his hand writing. His messy text sprawled across the page, written in haste so many years ago.

'My Dearest Vivienne,' it began. 'I don't have long to write. We're shipping out tomorrow but I can't tell you where. They say it's somewhere 'tropical'.'

She laughed a little. Tropical. She could sense his humour even through the page, and imagined how he would have smiled as he wrote the words she read. He had probably been told he was going somewhere warm and he's embellished the 'tropical'. A trait she fondly remembered of the storytelling soldier. She traced the paper with her old shaky fingers and her face crinkled in her momentary joy.

'The sun won't shine as bright as when I'm with you though Viv. Can't wait to get home and for you to make an honest man out of me.
Love you always
Carter.'

She scrunched the letter softly and held it close to her chest. Her slow ageing heart could still feel the skips of a young girl in love. She took a deep breath and released it gently.

'Do you still miss Grandpa Nan?' Missy asked tentatively. The bright eyed granddaughter mesmerised by her grandmother's quiet actions.

Viviene looked around the room. Wonderful memories filled the frames in which her small old house was adorned with. Her wedding, her children and their children. Her life was all around her. It was a good life. A happy life. She never cried anymore. It had been too long. The tears stopped flowing and a whole lifetime had passed.

'I do,' she answered sadly, as she picked up one of the frames and stared at the happy couple. Her hair once a strawberry blonde hue now as grey as her late husband's suit.

'Me too,' Missy replied with an exaggerated sigh. 'I really liked my poppy Jack.'

'I know,' Vivienne smiled. 'And hopefully one day you'll meet someone just like him.' She gazed back lovingly at the photograph. 'He'll show you a life you never could have imagined. And it will be beautiful.'

'Like a prince in a fairy-tale,' Missy cheerfully added, her blonde curls bobbing in her delight. Vivienne looked down again at her letter as she thought sadly, 'More like the knight after the prince had been slain by the dragon.'

She folded her letter from Carter once more, the familiar creases falling so easily into place.

'Can you read it to me?' Missy asked excitedly. 'No honey,' She smiled down at her granddaughter.

'Not today.'

'When?' the young girl asked anxiously.

Vivienne thought for a moment and smiled wisely. 'When you're old enough to hear two stories. One of what was, and one of what could have been.'

War with no Winners
Samuel Aubin

Some mornings I wake up and for a moment I am normal. For a moment I am living my life like it is meant to be lived. I do normal things. I make myself a cup of tea. I read the newspaper. I let the dog outside to go to the toilet.

Then something hits me like a clap of thunder in the distance. Loud and unexpected my world starts crashing down. It all comes flooding back to me like a raging river. There is no escape. There is no hiding from this thing that is my life. The life that was a new lottery ticket every day.

We have just returned from Afghanistan, from the battlefield of a war that has no winners.

I cannot forget the stench of blood.

I cannot forget the screams of fear.

I will not forget the sound of death, forever ringing in my ears.

The fear that is ubiquitous amongst us all.

Fear, fighting, fury, forever in my mind. I close my eyes and my memory takes me back to this place I call hell.

It is cold, it is morning and we are all wearisome. We can hear the pounding sound of machine guns firing in the distance. We soldiers scurry frantically like ants before a rainstorm. I can hear civilians screaming nearby. They are almost upon us.

This unexpected attack has taken us by surprise. We are neither ready nor prepared for this battle but know that it is inevitable. A bomb collides into the building next to us as if to remind us that this is real. I am thrown off my feet and for a moment think it may be best if I close my eyes and give up.

Another round of machine gun fire ricochets off my shoulder and snaps me back to reality. I manage to get to my feet. I notice then that my best friend is a casualty of this war that I have come to hate so much. This war that has no winners.

Mourning Bird

Judy Hooworth

Silently
out of the clear blue sky she returns.
Malicious grey bird
with weeping red eyes, cruel bill and
ash tipped wings . . .
her jet emblazoned talons glittering shards of silver.
Merciless
mourning bird.

She circles above then swoops
heading straight for my vulnerabilities
and tears a jagged opening
through already wounded flesh.

She enters by beak and claw
settling in
making a nest of the sticks and grasses of
uncertainty and despondency.
She might stay for a day, a week or more
uncertain whether or not to lay her
sorrow, anguish and remorse.
No sweet fluffy hatchlings here
only broken shells and runny embryos
smashed hopes and unfulfilled dreams . . .
they're all she can offer.

It's another uneasy nesting
and she preens
sheds some spiky feathers and lice
to remind me of her stay
spreads her weighty wings once more
and flies away.
The notes of her unsung song fall
like confetti
in the void..

We Remember Too . . .

Annika Leslie

I could see it then, as we came around the bend. The flashing blue and red from a lonely police car. The rhythmic flashes did nothing to slow the rapid beating of my anxious, nervous heart.

With my radio in place, my partner and I sprang from our ambulance. In the strange throbbing light we could make out the forms of two police officers. One hunched down over a small figure, the other with his hand to his chest and his mouth speaking soundless words.

I saw her then. She must have been not yet five years old. In the glow of our flashlight I could see her pale face, eyes open, a thin deep laceration on her cheek and a dirty, bloody graze on her forehead. Her hair was golden, the helmet askew and looked far too big—borrowed from an older sibling perhaps.

I dropped my kit down beside me as I knelt, my gloved hand darting towards her although I already knew there would be no pulse. I glanced at my partner and then at the police officer. Without a word, but a small nod we silently agreed that her broken little body could not be fixed.

I took off my gloves slowly. I looked down into those blue eyes and my own heart stopped for a moment as I noticed a single teardrop perched delicately on her eyelashes. Her blue eyes were now dull. Her full lips were grey. My eyes filled as I wiped her tear away and closed her eyes. The starry sky was the last thing she would have seen. Her face, along with the others, is the last thing I see every night . . .

Their house was lit up, several cars in the driveway and despite the gloom I could see a child, possibly an older sibling riding a bike up and down the footpath. The child looked up as we approached and politely directed us to the front door. A hint of a frown creasing his smooth forehead as he began to look around, searching.

My knuckles, white with stress, knocked on their dark wood door. The voices inside softened and footsteps approached. Automatically my left hand removed my police cap as a chink of light quickly widened to reveal a woman, her mouth drawn into a smile.

I saw her eyes sweep over us, recognizing our uniform and pausing as she noticed the hats in our hands. They widened then and she looked past us to her son and then began darting as she searched the darkened street for her daughter.

Her hand flew to her mouth as her knees sank to the floor. She took a ragged breath in through blood red lips and the sound that escaped her made me step back in shock. The sound echoes in my ears even now. The memories of all of those shrieks, cries, terrible racking, splintered sobs combine into one as I pour myself a drink . . . and then another.

What's the Score?
Anna McCormack

My father was a cricket buff from when he was a boy, sitting glued to the radio while they broadcasted The Test from Britain, stroke by stroke, run by run, complete with sound effects. He could tell you who had played whom, where and with what results over countless Test and One-Day cricket matches. If he'd gone in a television quiz program with special subject 'cricket', he'd have come out a millionaire. He had his heroes and followed the rise and fall of their cricketing careers avidly. Richie Benaud remained his number one.

'A real cricketer,' dad declared, making me wonder what all the other players were.

I had grown up with dad and his cricket. Not that he ever played much himself, just a bowl and bat with the local eleven, then back to listen to the real action on the radio, or, later, watch it on television. Even when no significant match was in progress, he would fill in time telling me of matches he'd seen in days long past. Me, I could take it or leave it.

As he grew older, chalking up the runs from septuagenarian to octogenarian then nonagenarian, his interest never waned, though his grasp on the reality of who was playing whom, where and with what results faltered.

'What's the score?' he would greet me, as I visited him every couple of days in the nursing home where he eventually lived.

I kept an eye on major games so that I could tell him about them, though now he wasn't sure who all these 'new blokes' were and was eternally puzzled by the absence of whites on the pitch. If nothing special was happening, I would make something up. He was always glad to know that Richie was Not Out.

One day, not long before his ninety-fourth birthday, he fell badly and the nursing home packed him off to hospital to be checked. He'd fallen before. Balancing his medications to keep him upright and alive was tricky. I caught up with him in Accident and Emergency, disconsolately tucked into a narrow white bed, straining to watch a battery of pinging screens over his shoulder.

'What's all that for?' he demanded. 'Nothing wrong with me. They say I fell but I don't remember.'

Here, he looked frailer, weaker than in his own room. With his knobbly bare shoulders, the white skin of his arms sagging dully, the chicken bones of his chest studded with sticky electrodes wired to the machines, he was a shadow of the man he had been. He knew it.

The doctors finished with him and decided to return him to the nursing home. One had a quiet word with me.

'It's only a matter of time,' he said.

Dad was watching me sharply as I turned from the doctor and started to help him dress. An orderly folded him into a wheelchair, ready to roll.

'What's the score?' dad asked.

'Ninety-four, not out,' I said.

He nodded, satisfied.

Why Don't Women Just Leave?
Laura Lee

I'd always wondered . . . until my feet started to fit 'those women's' shoes.

When our pet cockatiel squawked loudly in late afternoon we knew Daddy's car would be home two minutes later. I wondered, with a beating heart, which man ould turn the door handle.

Was it the man I'd married—who would plaster his young daughters with kisses and adoring smiles and tell me there was no need for the house to be so clean and tidy? Or the sullen tower ready to thunder out a bloodcurdling roar at them, arms flailing, for not picking up their toys? Would he have hugs and chuckles or a simmering coldness, boiling over into slamming fists, dark threats and things thrown?

Invisible bruises multiplied slowly in the darkness of our daughters' hearts.

'I worry about you and the girls,' were the quiet words of best friends. It was embarrassing to admit the secrets behind our walls, yet freeing to grieve with someone.

My soul ached to see his smile, to go for walks hand in hand with our girls skipping beside us.

Our eight-year-old now stuck to my side or withdrew to the shadows with her book, claiming she wasn't hungry. I awkwardly fumbled to soothe the children's tears after incidents. I felt I'd failed to give my children a safe home.

As I iced his favourite carrot cake I hoped the flavours would warm his heart. The sweetest icing didn't smooth things for long.

'He's such a lovely Dad,' were the admiring words of onlookers.

'He sounds tired and stressed from work,' said one. 'What do you think is making him this way?'

I had spent years trying to figure that out, dancing creatively around the eggshells underfoot. I grieved for his acceptance and love. Why weren't his girls and I enough for him?

'I think you and he have different perspectives,' said another after hearing his teary side of the story. She wouldn't have seen him turn on the tears as a party trick. I yearned to be believed, understood.

'I feel he's a ticking time bomb,' were the tired words of the Men's Behaviour Change counsellor, who'd originally been impressed with his voluntary participation. 'We have concerns for you and the children's safety. Think about getting an intervention order and safety plan.'

That sounded so dramatic. I didn't want to leave the man I loved. He hadn't always been like always this. There had been good times too.

I was scared to stay. My dreams for a whole and healthy family had disintegrated. The belief that he would change had faded away like crackling autumn leaves.

I was scared to leave too. How angry would that make him?

As I stumbled towards a new life, all I had left in that overwhelming grief was hope that there was still hope.

www.ingramcontent.com/pod-product-compliance
Lightning Source LLC
Chambersburg PA
CBHW050435010526
44118CB00013B/1530